PENGUIN BOOKS

KEYNES IN THE 1990s

Michael Stewart is Reader in Political Economy at University College London. He took first-class honours in Philosophy, Politics and Economics at Magdalen College, Oxford, and was subsequently Economic Adviser at the Treasury and Cabinet Office, and Senior Economic Adviser at 10 Downing Street. He has also served as Economic Adviser to the Kenya Treasury, and as Special Adviser to the Foreign and Commonwealth Secretary. He is the author of *Keynes and After*, also published by Penguin, *The Jekyll and Hyde Years: Politics and Economic Policy since 1964* and *Controlling the Economic Future: Policy Dilemmas in a Shrinking World*, and he is co-author of *Apocalypse 2000: Economic Breakdown and the Suicide of Democracy 1989–2000*. He twice stood as a Parliamentary Labour candidate, lives in Hampstead, and enjoys looking at paintings and eating in restaurants.

MICHAEL STEWART

KEYNES IN THE 1990s

A RETURN TO ECONOMIC SANITY

PENGUIN BOOKS

PENGUIN BOOKS

Published by the Penguin Group
Penguin Books Ltd, 27 Wrights Lane, London w8 5tz, England
Penguin Books USA Inc., 375 Hudson Street, New York, New York 10014, USA
Penguin Books Australia Ltd, Ringwood, Victoria, Australia
Penguin Books Canada Ltd, 10 Alcorn Avenue, Toronto, Ontario, Canada m4v 3b2
Penguin Books (NZ) Ltd, 182–190 Wairau Road, Auckland 10, New Zealand

Penguin Books Ltd, Registered Offices: Harmondsworth, Middlesex, England

First published 1993
3 5 7 9 10 8 6 4

Typeset by Datix International Limited, Bungay, Suffolk
Printed in England by Clays Ltd, St Ives plc

To David

CONTENTS

Acknowledgements   ix

1   THE HOUR OF MILTON FRIEDMAN   1

2   KEYNES AND UNEMPLOYMENT   11

3   INFLATION: FASHIONABLE STAGE VILLAIN   34

4   THE THATCHER EXPERIMENT: DOGMA AND DISASTER   47

5   THE ROLE OF THE BUDGET   71

6   STRENGTHENING THE SUPPLY SIDE   89

7   THE INTERNATIONAL CONTEXT   99

8   WHAT NOW?   119

    Index   127

ACKNOWLEDGEMENTS

I am much indebted to John Grieve Smith, Brian Lapping and Frances Stewart, all of whom read the initial typescript and made valuable suggestions for improvement; also to Wendy Carlin for comments on chapter 7 and Jo Nickolls for assistance in checking figures and quotations. None of them, of course, bears responsibility for any inadequacies in the final text.

June 1993

THE HOUR OF MILTON FRIEDMAN

The recession suffered by Britain in the early 1990s has been exceptionally severe.

Over the past twenty-five years the world has suffered four recessions, of varying degrees of duration and intensity. Two of them, in 1974–76 and 1980–83, were sparked by sudden, large increases in oil prices. The other two, that of 1970–72 and the one that began in 1990–91, were the products of more complex factors. All of them, however, were created or exacerbated by the policies of the G7 – the Group of Seven main industrial countries (the US, Japan, Germany, France, Britain, Italy and Canada), which between them account for nearly two-thirds of world output.

The accepted way of measuring the severity of a recession is to calculate the gap between actual output at the bottom of the recession and what output would have been if it had continued to grow in line with the long-term trend. Suppose that, on this basis, one were to rank the four recessions suffered in all the seven G7 countries since 1970 in ascending order of severity: of the twenty-eight national recessions listed, according to the Organization for Economic Cooperation and Development (OECD) (*Economic Outlook*, December 1992), the 1990–93 recession in Britain would rank second. Only the 1980–83 recession in Canada (much the smallest G7 country) has been worse. In other words, the recession which began in Britain – the birthplace of Keynesian economics – in 1990 is the worst that has been endured by any major country in the past twenty-five years.

How could this happen? What went wrong? What should be done – both to bring the country fully out of the present recession, and to ensure that nothing like it ever happens again? These are the questions this book seeks to answer. In the highly interdependent world in which we now live, part of the answer lies in decisions and developments abroad, over which Britain has no control; this international dimension is discussed in chapter 7. But even today, what happens to the British economy is mainly the consequence of policies adopted in Britain. British governments cannot hide behind what is happening in other countries. The buck stops here.

For a quarter of a century after the end of the Second World War unemployment in Britain averaged less than 2 per cent. Since 1970 it has averaged more than three times that – and appears to be on a rising trend: it averaged 4 per cent in the 1970s and 10 per cent in the 1980s. It rose steadily throughout 1991 and 1992, and by the beginning of 1993 was over 10 per cent, or 3 million. However, after 1979 various changes were made in the way that unemployment was measured, which had the effect of reducing the figures significantly. If unemployment were still measured as it was in 1979, it would have been over 12 per cent at the beginning of 1993.

To a rational observer surveying the scene in 1970, what has happened during the ensuing couple of decades would have been beyond belief. For it seemed then that the Keynesian revolution had put paid for good to the kind of mass unemployment that Britain had suffered in the 1920s and, even more, the 1930s. The idea that in the early 1990s the rate of unemployment would be back in double figures, that bankruptcies would be shutting up shops and erecting 'For Sale' signs outside factories in every town in Britain, that tens of thousands of families would be evicted from the homes they thought they owned because they could no longer service their mortgages – all this would have seemed strange indeed: it must be another country; it couldn't happen here.

There was, to be sure, one cloud on the horizon in 1970. Inflation, which had averaged about 4 per cent a year during the twenty-five years since 1945, was beginning to creep up: it was over 5 per cent in 1969 and over 6 per cent in 1970. But this could be explained by one-off factors. One was the inflationary impact around the world, in the later 1960s, of America's simultaneous attempts to fight an escalating war in Vietnam and create Lyndon Johnson's Great Society at home. Another was the effect on Britain's import prices of the 1967 devaluation of sterling – made necessary, under the Bretton Woods fixed exchange-rate regime, by the fact that although Britain's inflation rate was quite low, other countries' were even lower, and British goods had become increasingly uncompetitive. A third factor was the spectacular Paris *événements* of May 1968, which culminated in inflationary wage rises in France and other European countries, including Britain.

Despite these worries about inflation, the notion enshrined in the Coalition government's famous 1944 White Paper *Employment Policy* – that the government both could and should maintain full employment – persisted well into the 1970s. This was demonstrated by Mr Edward Heath's famous U-turn. Elected in June 1970, his Conservative government started off with a good deal of anti-inflationary rhetoric about resisting public-sector pay claims and refusing to bail out 'lame-duck' industries, even if this refusal led to job losses – as it did. Unemployment, which had been flat at $2\frac{1}{2}$ per cent throughout 1970, started to rise quite rapidly. By mid-1971 it was $3\frac{1}{2}$ per cent, and it looked as though by early 1972 it would be nudging 4 per cent, or, in absolute numbers, what was then regarded as the politically explosive figure of 1 million. In consequence, between July 1971 and March 1972 the Chancellor, Mr Anthony Barber, initiated an increasingly desperate series of expansionary measures designed to stabilize and then reduce unemployment, regardless of the effects they might have on inflation (and the balance of payments). The rights and wrongs of the 'Barber boom' have been much debated, as have those of its successor, the 'Lawson boom' of the late 1980s: there is some discussion of these booms later in the book. For present purposes, however, the point is that even as long after the war as the early 1970s full employment was still regarded as the most important objective of economic policy, to be pursued vigorously even if it meant tolerating an inflation rate of perhaps 6 or 7 per cent a year.

How long this laid-back attitude would have persisted if inflation had stayed at this sort of level is impossible to say because, before long, the inflation rate was in double figures and still rising. There were a number of identifiable reasons for this, in addition to the undoubted fact that Barber's measures un-leashed a much bigger rise in spending than the economy's productive capacity could cope with. One was the near-doubling of some world commodity prices in 1972–3 because of rapid growth of manufacturing output, and hence the demand for primary products, in the industrial countries; and poor North American and Russian harvests. Another was the quadrupling of oil prices by the Organization of Petroleum Exporting Coun-tries (OPEC) in 1973–4. A third was the huge wage increases in Britain in 1974–5 following the destruction of the Heath govern-ment by the 1973–4 miners' strike.

However well the phenomenon could be explained, the unfortu-nate fact was that by mid-1975 the annual inflation rate in Britain was over 25 per cent, and millions of people dependent on savings, or living on fixed (or even just slowly rising) incomes, faced ruin. There was panic in the air. One suspects that it was at around this time that a great many people in Britain came to two conclusions. One was that the most important economic objective was to get inflation right down and keep it down – never mind about full employment. The other was that anyone who managed to smash the power of the unions would get their gratitude and, much more important, their vote. The conse-quences of this sea-change in attitudes are with us still.

Before long the prayers of millions were answered. On to centre stage, from the wings where they had been waiting rest-lessly and increasingly vocally, marched Milton Friedman and the monetarists. There was nothing particularly new about monetarism, a doctrine long associated with the University of Chicago: Friedman had been propounding his version of it since the 1950s, and there was much of the nineteenth century about it. But cometh the hour, cometh the man, and in the mid-1970s Friedman's hour had come.

Milton Friedman's views are discussed more fully in chapter 2. In essence, his argument was that inflation is caused by too rapid a growth of the stock of money, or 'money supply'. If this grew faster than the real output of the economy, the difference would take the form of an increase in prices. A major cause of an excessive growth of the money supply – pretty well the only

4

cause, in the view of some of his British disciples, including Mr Nigel Lawson, Chancellor of the Exchequer from 1983 to 1989 – was a government budget deficit. If a government finances such a deficit by borrowing from the banking system (what is sometimes called 'printing money' – a vivid but inaccurate phrase, since nowadays money consists mainly of bank deposits, not bank notes), the money supply will rise, and the result will be inflation. The moral was simple. To avoid inflation, the government must balance its budget and control the growth of the money supply.

Monetarism had already made considerable headway in the United States, and it began to have a major impact in Britain and other European countries in the mid-1970s. Both the Labour Prime Minister (James Callaghan) and Chancellor of the Exchequer (Denis Healey) appear to have been converted to the new faith, though there may have been an element of convenience in this: in 1976 the government needed to borrow money from the International Monetary Fund, where many of the doctrine's most fervent disciples were to be found. Whether or not monetarism was still only trundling along the runway under Labour, there was no doubt that it got well and truly airborne under Mrs Thatcher. She had already embraced the new creed with the fervour of a medieval zealot; now, as she took office in May 1979, she was able to start putting what she had preached into practice.

For a while it seemed to work brilliantly. Inflation had come down from 26 per cent in 1975 to less than 10 per cent in 1979 – though more because of the Labour government's prices and incomes policy (which used the law to reduce the size of wage and price increases) than because of its application of monetarism. In 1980, after Mrs Thatcher's arrival in power, there was a brief inflationary blip, to over 20 per cent, partly because there had been inflationary wage and price increases in the pipeline in 1979, partly in consequence of the second oil shock, and partly because the new Conservative government increased VAT from 8 per cent to 15 per cent, which in itself added 4 per cent to the retail price index. But after 1980, as monetarist policies were pursued, the inflation rate fell dramatically, down to a level of less than 3 per cent in 1986. The government duly took, and kept on taking, a bow for saving the nation from disaster. Monetarism had clearly triumphed.

Or had it? It did not require the talents of a Sherlock Holmes to see that the official version left some crucial evidence unexplained. At the heart of the monetarist approach was the assertion of a close correlation between the money supply and the price level. If, mainly because of technological progress, the total output of the British economy could rise by about 3 per cent a year, then a stable price level (a zero inflation rate) would be achieved by keeping the money supply rising by 3 per cent a year. But between 1980 and 1986 the government's own preferred measure of the money supply ('sterling M3') proved far harder to control than the monetarists had suggested, and rose at an average rate of no less than 17 per cent a year. So, according to monetarist doctrine, inflation in 1986 should have been around 14 per cent. Yet it was less than 3 per cent – a figure that was, of course, very welcome, but which could hardly be explained by monetarism. For the doctrine's adherents it was all a bit embarrassing.

The real cause of the steep decline in inflation between 1980 and 1986 was not difficult to find. Part of it lay in a fall of about a third in world commodity prices because of the world recession; this must have had a favourable impact on inflation in Britain, even though much of it was offset by a fall of about a quarter in the international value of sterling. But a much more important reason was that between 1980 and 1986 unemployment rose from less than 1.5 million to well over 3 million. Steeply rising unemployment obviously exercises a dampening effect on inflation. Workers, afraid they may lose their jobs tomorrow, are circumspect in their demands for higher pay. Employers, fearing collapsing profits or even bankruptcy, cut their costs and cut their prices. The result is a fall in the inflation rate.

This large and prolonged rise in unemployment was another embarrassment for the monetarists, because it had not been in the script. Friedman himself, giving evidence to a House of Commons committee in 1980, had said that the rise in unemployment resulting from the application of his policies would be modest and temporary, and that the effect on investment and the potential for future growth would be highly favourable. The fact that unemployment went on rising for much longer, and reached a much higher level, than Milton Friedman and her other economic gurus had led her to expect did not seem to trouble Mrs Thatcher unduly ('U-turn if you want,' as she had told the Tory wets at the party conference at Blackpool in 1980, 'the lady's not for turning.') OK, her attitude seemed to be, maybe unemployment has risen a bit more than we expected, but that's because our measures to restore the supremacy of market forces – reducing the powers of the unions, privatizing nationalized industries and so forth – haven't yet been completed. We've got inflation right down – and we're going to press on until we get it down to zero; and now that inflationary expectations have been squeezed out of the system, labour markets will adjust, unemployment will come down to its natural rate, and we will embark on a path of steady, long-term, non-inflationary growth.

All this sounded splendid, but you did not need to be Aristotle to see that there was something wrong with the logic. If the main reason for the dramatic fall in inflation in the first half of the 1980s had been the equally dramatic rise in unemployment, then what would happen when unemployment stopped rising – or when, as Mrs Thatcher claimed would happen, it started to fall? Similarly, what would happen when world commodity prices stopped falling and started to rise? In short, if both these factors went into reverse, might not the fall in inflation go into reverse as well?

And so, of course, it turned out. Unemployment did start falling in 1986, and from a peak of over 11 per cent (on the new, government-friendly, definition – over 13 per cent on the old definition) it fell to less than 6 per cent in 1990. Correspondingly, world commodity prices did start rising in 1986 and were up by about a third by 1990. And inflation? Inflation rose every year, from less than 3 per cent in 1986 to more than 10 per cent in 1990. The dragon had not been slain after all.

An element in this resurgence of inflation was, to be sure, the irresponsible monetary and fiscal policies pursued by the Chancellor of the Exchequer (Mr Nigel Lawson) in 1987–8. There was less excuse for the Lawson boom than for the Barber boom fifteen years earlier, partly because the Barber boom was there as a salutary warning, and partly because Mr Barber had had no pretensions to understanding the workings of the economy, whereas Mr Lawson rather fancied himself in this capacity, having once written on economic matters for the *Financial Times* and other newspapers, and having been the main architect, within the government, of the 'Medium Term Financial Strategy' (MTFS) that dominated policymaking in the early 1980s. In general, Mr Lawson's conduct as Chancellor demonstrated a degree of *hubris* which made many observers feel the *nemesis* that eventually overtook him to be entirely fitting. Nevertheless, Mr Lawson's errors of timing and judgement merely made things a little worse, a little sooner. For it was the government's fundamental approach to the running of the economy that was wrong.

This the government entirely failed to perceive. Its response to the double-digit inflation rate that confronted it in 1990 was not discernibly different from its response to the same phenomenon ten years earlier. Inflation, it declared, was an evil that must be defeated at all costs. The way to do this was to control the money supply, and the way to control the money supply was to keep interest rates as high as necessary for as long as necessary (at least this was an advance: at the beginning of the 1980s it had been supposed that the money supply could be controlled directly, like controlling the flow of water from a tap). Rising unemployment was, regrettably, an unavoidable by-product of the high interest rates needed to squeeze inflation out of the system. 'If the policy isn't hurting, it isn't working,' declared the Chancellor of the Exchequer (Mr John Major) on 27 October 1989. To conquer inflation 'unemployment is a price well worth paying,' stated his successor as Chancellor (Mr Norman Lamont) on 16 May 1991.

So history started to repeat itself. Inflation fell rapidly during 1991, to less than 5 per cent by the end of the year, and continued to fall, though more slowly, during 1992. Meanwhile unemployment started to rise, and went on rising inexorably. From less than 6 per cent in the middle of 1990, it had risen to 9 per cent by the end of 1991 and was over 10 per cent (over 12 per cent on the old definition) by early 1993. Increasingly (because of over-borrowing for house purchase in the late 1980s) people lost not only their jobs but their homes as well. Output fell; investment fell; firms went bankrupt. It was just like old times. And a few observers with long memories began to wonder whether the old times in question might not be the early 1930s rather than the early 1980s.

Although there were striking similarities between the early 1980s and the early 1990s, there were also fundamental differences, few of them favourable. Quite big productivity gains were achieved in British industry in the early 1980s as overmanning was reduced and weaker firms went to the wall; there was much less scope for this in the early 1990s. At the beginning of the 1980s North Sea oil was just starting to come to the rescue of the balance of payments, and by 1985 there was an export surplus on fuel of over £6 billion; by 1991 the fuel balance was back in deficit. The weakening in the balance of payments as a whole, from healthy surpluses in the early 1980s to big (sometimes very big) deficits in the late 1980s and early 1990s, was even more pronounced.

The most striking difference of all, however, was the most obvious one. At the beginning of the 1980s the monetarist experiment was only just getting under way and, however implausible its assumptions, there was no conclusive way of demonstrating that it was not the answer. Ten years later it had been tried, and it had manifestly failed. Whatever else the decade had seen, it had not seen a relatively painless transition to a utopia of low inflation, low unemployment and steady growth.

Yet nothing seemed to have been learned. The policies that failed in the 1980s were doggedly pursued in the early 1990s, to the accompaniment of the endlessly chanted mantra that first of all inflation must be eliminated and then all would be well.

As the state of the British economy has grown ever more parlous over the last few years, alibis aplenty have been offered, scapegoats galore identified. It is all the fault of the American recession, the collapse of the Japanese stock market, the Bundesbank, the Exchange Rate Mechanism (ERM), the (first) Danish referendum on Maastricht – never the fault of British economic policymakers. Their task is, of course, complicated by decisions and events in other countries, but this has been true for a long time. A British government has less freedom of action than it had thirty or forty years ago, when it had a battery of direct controls (including import and exchange controls) at its disposal; but it is not necessarily less free than it was ten or fifteen years ago. And the fact is that economic policy, like charity, begins at home. Clearly, by the early 1990s economic policy in Britain had reached a dead end. It was fundamentally wrong and needed to be changed. But, until September 1992, no signs of change were discernible.

Suddenly, in September 1992, the government made a U-turn. The change of direction was so sudden and so total as to make the average observer dizzy. It was as if he had been consulting the signposts at a crossroads, then blinked and found that the signs were all pointing in a different direction. We shall come back to the causes and consequences of this U-turn in chapter 4.

2

KEYNES AND UNEMPLOYMENT

Adam Smith, whose *Wealth of Nations* was published in 1776, was the father of modern economics. He argued, in effect, that the unfettered operation of market forces was the best recipe for a thriving and growing economy. If everyone is as free as possible to pursue his own self-interest, he will be led by an 'invisible hand' to promote the welfare of society as a whole. Smith's analysis was much extended and refined in the nineteenth century by David Ricardo and John Stuart Mill, and later by Alfred Marshall and others, and came to be described as 'classical economics'. Since the essence of this classical economics was that market forces would ensure that resources were fully utilized and optimally allocated, what later came to be called 'full employment' was regarded as the normal state of affairs, to which the economy naturally gravitated. This did not, of course, mean that there was never anywhere any unemployment. In a dynamic, growing economy a host of factors – the invention of new products or techniques of production, the opening up of new markets or sources of supply abroad, shifts in taste or fashion – meant that jobs were continually being lost in particular industries or occupations. But this process also meant that other jobs were continually being created. Labour would move from declining industries, where wages were falling and jobs being lost, to expanding ones, where wages were rising and jobs being created. The process would not be completely instantaneous or painless, and from time to time unemployment would appear, sometimes just in particular areas, sometimes more generally. But this unemployment was temporary and transitional, and would soon be eliminated by the normal operation of market forces.

This account of how the market economy worked had remarkable staying power. Among other things, it survived the experience of the trade cycle. This was a fairly regular phenomenon in the nineteenth century, typically taking a decade or so to come full circle, with perhaps four or five years of rising output and employment (and wages and prices) being succeeded by a plateau and then a few years of falling output and employment (and wages and prices). Unemployment might be as low as 1 or 2 per cent at the top of the boom, but would then rise to 8 or 10 per cent at the bottom of the recession. But because, after a year or two, unemployment would start falling again as the economy enjoyed a new burst of expansion, the implicit belief that full employment was the normal state of affairs remained quite easy to sustain – particularly on the part of the thinking and writing classes not themselves subject to periodic bouts of unemployment. By the end of the 1920s, however, a decade in which unemployment in Britain had averaged 11 per cent, the comforting assumption that the economy was self-stabilizing at full employment was beginning to look more than a little threadbare. By the end of the 1930s, a decade in which unemployment averaged 16 per cent, it looked positively obscene.

In 1936 the whole classical model of how the economy worked was challenged – one might reasonably say overthrown – by the publication of John Maynard Keynes's *General Theory of Employment, Interest and Money*. Once they had been absorbed, Keynes's theory and its implications dominated economic policy-making for a third of a century. It is a pity that it was not two thirds of a century.

In order to understand the revolutionary nature of Keynes's theory, it may be helpful if, first of all, the classical theory it displaced is briefly set out – not in the way in which it was discussed in the nineteenth century, but in the terminology that grew out of Keynes's work and is now in everyday use. To avoid unnecessary complexity it is assumed, in the main, that the economy is closed (i.e. that it has no dealings with other countries) and that income is divided into only two categories, wages and profits.

The total *output* of the economy is the same thing as the total *income* of the economy and the total *expenditure* of the economy. This total is called the Gross Domestic Product (GDP). Incomes, in the form of wages and profits, are derived from the process of creating output, and these incomes are spent on the goods and services created. In a given year (making allowances for any change there may be in the level of stocks) total incomes, total output and total expenditure must be equal. In effect, the classical economists assumed that the GDP would always be at full employment – i.e. that incomes, output and expenditure would all be at the maximum level permitted by the country's labour force and stock of capital equipment.

It was Thomas Malthus (better known for his prognostications of over-population, now frighteningly topical) who first raised the worry that was later to be taken up by Keynes. What if, he said, people did not spend all their income, but saved some of it? Then surely there would be a 'general glut of commodities', and output and employment would fall. Not so, replied Ricardo and the other classical economists. If income was not spent on *consumer* goods (food and clothing), it would be spent on *investment* or *capital* goods (factories and machines).

Look at it this way, said the classical economists. Total incomes could be regarded as either being spent on consumption, thus providing a living to the manufacturers of consumer goods, or saved. But these savings would be invested, thus providing a living for the makers of investment or capital goods as well. The investment might be done by the same people who did the saving – notably businessmen, out of their undistributed profits. In this case there would be no problem: all businessmen's income that was not spent on consumer goods would be automatically spent on capital goods, and (making the reasonable assumption that wages were so low they would all be spent on consumption) in this way one could be sure that all the income generated by a full employment level of output would be spent on that output, thus guaranteeing continued full employment.

It might be, on the other hand, that saving and investment were done by different groups of people. This was increasingly the case as the nineteenth century proceeded. Real wages grew, thus permitting workers to do some saving, and firms expanded, needing more capital to finance investment than they could provide from their own profits. How, in this more complicated case, could one be sure that all the savings generated by a fully employed economy would be automatically invested, thus ensuring that all the goods produced would find a buyer and that full employment would be maintained?

Easy, said the classical economists. Market forces will take care of it; leave it to the price mechanism. Any tendency for saving to exceed investment – or, to employ a later but useful piece of terminology, any tendency for the supply of 'loanable funds' to exceed the demand for these funds – will lead to a fall in the rate of interest. This fall in the rate of interest will make saving less attractive, thus reducing the supply of loanable funds (and raising the level of consumers' expenditure). At the same time it will make investment more attractive, since businesses can now borrow at lower cost, so the demand for loanable funds (and the level of investment) will rise. In short, the price mechanism – in this case taking the form of the rate of interest – will ensure that all the savings generated by a fully employed economy are automatically invested, and this will in turn guarantee the continuation of full employment.

This story was thoroughly satisfying, for it explained how saving and investment were brought into equality with each other, even though they were done by different groups of people. And saving and investment *had* to be equal, because the total income of the economy is the same thing as the total expenditure of the economy. *Saving* is the difference between income and consumption. *Investment* is that portion of total expenditure which is devoted to investment goods and not consumer goods. Since total income and total expenditure are equal, it follows that saving must equal investment. (This applies to a closed economy. In an open economy it is different, since a country may borrow from abroad, thus investing more than it saves, or lend abroad, thus investing less than it saves. These complications do not affect the basic argument.)

However, although the story might be thoroughly satisfying, according to Keynes it was at best a special case, describing a world that, if it had ever existed, certainly existed no longer. As an account of how a twentieth-century economy worked it was simply wrong.

Let us consider Keynes's criticism of the classical account of how changes in the rate of interest brought saving and investment into balance and thus ensured the maintenance of full employment.

Suppose (keeping it very simple, as before) that one starts with a fully employed economy, in which workers are spending, say, 90 per cent of their incomes on consumption and saving the rest. These savings arc lent (through the financial markets – perhaps in the form of contributions to occupational pension schemes) to businesses, which use them to finance investment. Assuming that businesses are also using all their own profits to finance investment in new buildings, plant and machinery, etc., it is clear that all of the income, both wages and profits, generated by a fully employed economy is being spent on either the consumer goods or the investment goods that the economy is producing. Thus incomes, expenditure and output are all at their maximum level, which ensures full employment.

Now suppose that for some reason – a widespread fear that rainy days are on the way, for example – workers suddenly decide to increase their saving to 20 per cent of their incomes. According to the classical theory, as we have seen, this would lead to a fall in interest rates, discouraging saving and encouraging investment. As interest rates are lower than they expected, workers might decide to save only 15 per cent of their incomes, and businesses will invest more than they had planned to, now that they can borrow more cheaply. The interest rate will fall to precisely that point at which saving and investment are equal. The economy will still be fully employed, but output will take the form of rather fewer consumer goods (because workers are now consuming only 85 per cent of their incomes) and rather more investment goods (because businesses are now investing more). That is the classical story.

According to Keynes, what happens is quite different. The workers' decision to increase their saving from 10 per cent of their incomes to 20 per cent is also a decision to reduce their consumption by a little over 10 per cent (from 90 per cent of their income to 80 per cent). This cut in their consumption expenditure will lead to a fall in the output of consumer goods and hence in the incomes and employment of those who make them. These people will now have less to spend and will cut their consumption, leading to further falls in output, incomes and employment elsewhere in the economy. What Keynes (borrowing from Richard Kahn) called a *multiplier* will be at work: the initial fall in consumers' expenditure will be much multiplied as falling expenditure leads to falling incomes, and falling incomes lead to falling expenditure, and so on – not quite *ad infinitum*, but a long way. (In the above example, where workers decided to save 20 per cent, or one-fifth, of their income, it can be shown – assuming for simplicity that profits and investment remain unchanged – that the multiplier would be five. In other words, the fall in the GDP would be five times as great as the initial fall in consumers' expenditure. In practice, the multiplier will be smaller than this, partly because it is damped down by the existence of taxes and partly because, in an open economy, some of the impact of declining expenditure falls on imports and not on domestic output and employment.)

The crucial point about this analysis is that it is not *interest rates* but *incomes* that adjust in a way that ensures that saving and investment are equal. And if incomes (and thus output and employment) have to fall a long way in order to establish a stable equilibrium between saving and investment, then unemployment may rise to a high level and *stay there*. This, said Keynes, is not just what could happen; it is what did happen – in the 1920s in Britain, and in the 1930s in most of the rest of the world as well.

This piece of analysis is so important that it deserves to be emphasized. It was pointed out earlier that saving and investment have to be equal, because they both represent income minus consumption. But if the decision on how much to save is taken mainly by millions of workers, whereas the decision on how much to invest is taken mainly by thousands of businesses, how can it be that the two figures turn out to be exactly equal? In the classical model this equality was brought about by changes in the rate of interest at an unchanged, full employment level of output. Keynes's explanation was different. If, for example, workers *want* to save a different amount from what businesses *want* to invest, the GDP will change until what workers want to save will be the same as what businesses want to invest. In the above example, there was initially an equilibrium in which workers wanted to save, and did save, 10 per cent of their incomes, and this amount (plus business profits) was the same as what businesses wanted to invest, and did invest. Everything was fine. Then workers suddenly upset the applecart by deciding to increase their saving to 20 per cent of their incomes. Unless businesses simultaneously decide to increase their investment correspondingly (which is improbable, given the reduced demand for consumer goods), the new situation will be that workers want to save more than businesses want to invest. Since by definition this outcome cannot occur, what will happen is that workers' incomes will fall, via the operation of the multiplier, until they get to the level at which the 20 per cent of them that the workers save will (together with profits) be equal to the (by assumption unchanged) amount that businesses want to invest. The workers' higher *propensity* to save will not have led to any change in their actual saving, because they are now saving a higher proportion of a lower income.

The analysis would have proceeded in exactly the same way if we had looked at the other side of the equation, and considered a sudden fall in business investment. Unless the fall in the amount that businesses decided to invest was for some reason offset by a fall in the amount that workers wanted to save – so that the GDP stayed at full employment, but with a larger output of consumer goods and a smaller output of investment goods – the GDP would fall until a new equilibrium was established. At this new equilibrium the smaller amount that businesses wanted to invest would be exactly matched (after taking account of the investment financed out of profits) by the amount that workers wanted to save. Workers would, by assumption, be saving the same proportion of their incomes as at the beginning, but their total saving would be smaller because their incomes would be lower.

To summarize: saving and investment have to be equal to each other, but according to Keynes what brings this equality about is not changes in interest rates at an unchanged level of employment, but changes in the level of the GDP. The new equilibrium level of GDP may be one at which there is high unemployment, and this equilibrium may persist for a long time.

There is another way in which the nineteenth century classical economists explained how full employment was maintained. If there is unemployment, the argument went, it is because wages are too high. Workers are asking for more than the value of their output, so naturally no employer will take them on. Market forces – competition between workers – will ensure that wages fall to the level at which employers find it profitable to give them jobs. Of course, this process will be impeded if trade unions prevent competition between workers from driving wages down to the level required to maintain full employment. But if that does not happen, and workers agree to work for lower wages, they will all find a job.

It all sounds reasonable enough. But it is not so simple. If one worker agrees to work for less than the going wage, he is indeed likely to find a job. But if all workers agree to do this, the outcome will be a reduction in consumption and investment throughout the economy.

Suppose (again, in a closed economy) that there is heavy unemployment and that workers have been diligently studying the classical economics of the late nineteenth century (or, for that matter, the monetarist economics of the late twentieth century). Suddenly light dawns. If they agree to, say, a 10 per cent wage cut, from £300 a week to £270, everyone will find a job. Full employment will be restored.

Alas, not so, according to Keynes. He sees two possibilities. The first is that even though wages are reduced, prices remain the same. This ought to make output more profitable to the employer. But to whom will this output be sold? With a 10 per cent cut in money wages but no change in prices, workers' *real* wages will have fallen by 10 per cent, and they are likely to cut their consumption accordingly. And consumers' expenditure accounts for 60–70 per cent of the GDP. Thus, in the absence of an offsetting rise in investment, which is improbable, the GDP, and hence employment, will fall, not rise. Wage reductions, supposed to reduce unemployment, have increased it.

The second possibility – and the one that Keynes considered more likely – is that if there is a 10 per cent reduction in money wages (across the whole economy), there will also be something like a 10 per cent reduction in prices, since in general, in a modern industrial economy characterized by large (often multinational) corporations, prices are determined by adding a mark-up to unit costs, of which wages are the most important component. But if there is a 10 per cent reduction in prices, there will have been no change in *real* wages because, although money wages are now only 90 per cent of what they were, they will buy the same amount as before. And if there is no change in *real* wages, then according to the classical economists' own analysis there is no reason to expect any change in employment. In short, reductions in money wages will not reduce unemployment.

It would thus appear that, in the closed-economy case, market forces cannot be relied on to maintain or restore full employment through the flexibility of wages, any more than they can be relied on to do this through the variability of interest rates. (In an open economy it is a different story, since the level of wages can affect international competitiveness. This matter comes up again, quite often, later in the book.) The conclusion that Keynes drew from this analysis was that market forces are not enough. Wage cuts are not the answer to unemployment. There are times when the only answer is substantial intervention by the government.

Keynes by no means ruled out the possibility that this intervention could take the form of monetary policy – a reduction in interest rates. But in the context of the heavy unemployment of the 1930s he did not think this could be of much help. For various reasons, mainly connected with *expectations* (a subject about which he knew a great deal more than most of those who now endlessly chatter about it in the financial markets), Keynes did not believe that it was feasible to get interest rates down to a low enough level to tempt businesses to borrow and invest. At a time when there was already a lot of existing capacity standing idle, and the outlook for sales was grim, businesses would be reluctant to take the risk of installing more capacity, which might stand idle as well.

If monetary policy is ineffective as a way of getting a heavily unemployed economy back to work, then (still considering a closed economy) the answer has to be fiscal policy. To Keynes's mind, what was needed in this situation was either a large increase in government expenditure on public works, or a reduction in taxes – especially on the less well-off, who spend most or all of their income – so that consumers' expenditure would rise. In general, it was the former of these that he favoured. By spending money on what would now be called the infrastructure, the government would directly create employment for large numbers of people. They in turn would spend the incomes they were now earning, so that – with the multiplier now operating in an expansionary rather than a contractionary direction – the whole economy would be lifted back up to full employment.

Of course, this policy would require the abandonment, at any rate in the short run, of the age-old shibboleth of a balanced budget. It would be no good financing extra government expenditure by raising taxes – that would just be taking away with one hand what was being given by the other, and the net expansionary effect on the economy would be nil, or close to it. The extra government expenditure would have to be financed by borrowing, either from the banking system or by sales of government securities to the non-bank public. But that, said Keynes, did not matter: the important thing was to balance not the government's budget but the economy as a whole. The extra employment, output and income resulting from this kind of expansionary fiscal policy would much outweigh in importance the budget deficit that would, at any rate in the short run, be one of its consequences.

In an open economy an increase in exports – if imports are unchanged – will have the same kind of expansionary effects as an increase in government expenditure, if taxes are unchanged. For a country like Britain, which has been plagued by balance- of-payments difficulties throughout the post-war period, an increase in exports, particularly at a time of recession, is a consummation devoutly to be wished. But it is not easy to arrange. Unlike its own expenditure and tax rates, which it controls, the government's influence on exports, which depend both on the country's competitiveness and on what is happening to world trade, is limited. The issue of the relationship between Britain's exports and imports will be discussed in later chapters.

From Keynes's theory of how the economy worked, governments have since developed the art of *demand management*. According to this, the government, far from leaving everything to market forces, must attempt to assess whether over the next year or two there is going to be enough *effective demand* in the economy to maintain full employment. ('Effective demand' has no truck with window-shopping, wishful thinking or burglary; it is demand backed by money – i.e. actual expenditure.) If projected expenditure by consumers, businesses and the government itself looks like adding up to less than the economy can produce, the government will stimulate effective demand by increasing its own expenditures or reducing taxes, even if this means a budget deficit. If, on the other hand, demand looks like being too high for the economy to cope with, thus posing an inflationary threat, the government will cut its own expenditure or increase taxes, even if this means a budget surplus. (It is interesting to note that the first British budget in which the aim was not to balance the budget itself, but to secure an appropriate level of effective demand, was of this latter kind: formulated under the influence of the pamphlet *How to pay for the war*, which Keynes had written in 1940, the 1941 budget aimed to *reduce* effective demand in the economy in order to release resources for the war effort.)

After the war demand management was deliberately and continuously practised for some thirty years, a period during which unemployment averaged about 2 per cent and economic growth about 2¾ per cent a year. Only in the later 1970s did its hold on economic policymaking start to weaken, and only in 1979, with the advent of Mrs Thatcher, was it finally jettisoned altogether.

In the United States, after the stagnation of the Eisenhower years in the later 1950s, demand management was vigorously used by the Kennedy administration and over-vigorously by Kennedy's successor, Johnson, who allowed domestic pressures arising from his Great Society programme to be piled on top of the escalating burden of the war in Vietnam. The consequent over-heating of the American economy had inflationary consequences around the world. (Demand management is much more difficult to practise in the United States than in Britain because monetary policy is the province of the independent Federal Reserve Board, and fiscal policy is something of a shuttle-cock, being for ever batted up and down Pennsylvania Avenue. Even when the White House and the Congress are controlled by the same party there can be difficulties: early in 1993 the newly elected Democratic President Clinton found it impossible to get a very modest stimulative tax package through the Democratic-controlled Senate. In Britain, by contrast, a government with a majority in the House of Commons can expect to put a coherent economic policy into effect immediately and without difficulty – assuming that it is capable of formulating such a policy.)

In other countries, such as France and Germany, less was heard about demand management in the decades after the war, but this was more because the deliberate manipulation of demand was unnecessary than because the philosophy as such was rejected. In Germany, for much of the post-war period, the currency was undervalued, and thus exports were very competitive: the rapid growth of exports, and the high level of manufacturing investment this stimulated, of themselves created a high level of effective demand in the country. In France a similar role was played for many years by large-scale, carefully planned, long-term pro-grammes of government spending on the economic infrastructure, which went ahead regardless of short-term ups and downs in the budgetary situation.

The cases of these two countries, during the first two or three decades after the war, illustrate a key feature of demand manage-ment. This is that the government undertakes to ensure that there is enough effective demand in the economy to maintain full employment (but not so much as to create inflationary pressures). If decisions by individuals and businesses to consume or not to consume, to invest or not to invest, of themselves create an adequate level of effective demand, well and good: no change in fiscal or monetary policy is required. But if they do not, then the government must take action, and if this results in a budget deficit, so be it.

*

One can identify a number of reasons why demand management fell from grace during the 1970s, and was consigned to outer darkness by Mrs Thatcher in 1979. All of them are connected in one way or another with the shift that took place in the 1970s, away from the idea that low unemployment was the most important objective of government policy, in favour of the idea that low inflation was.

One experience that undoubtedly discredited demand management was the 'Barber boom'. In an attempt, praiseworthy in itself, to prevent a continuing rise in unemployment, the increasingly panicky Chancellor of the Exchequer, Mr Anthony Barber, introduced between July 1971 and March 1972 a series of expansionary measures that included cuts in income tax and purchase tax, increases in public expenditure, the abolition of hire-purchase controls and a major relaxation of monetary policy. Some of these measures were taken, fatally, before previous ones could possibly have had time to have an effect. The consequence was predictable (though by only a few actually predicted). From late 1972 onwards all these individual measures coalesced into a raging torrent of rising demand, far greater than the economy's productive capacity could cope with. The balance of payments crashed into heavy deficit, and inflation mounted alarmingly. It could be argued that the Barber boom was a judgement not on demand management as such, but on an over-ambitious refinement of it, sometimes known as 'fine tuning', which assumes that detailed knowledge of the state of the economy, and exactly how it functions, is more accurate than it is, and accordingly claims that the economy can be nudged along in the right direction by making minor adjustments to policy instruments every quarter or even every month. But this nice distinction could not be expected to cut much ice outside the seminar room; the fact remains that the Barber boom gave demand management a bad name.

Another criticism of demand management – and in many ways it was a justified criticism – was that the way in which it had been operated, particularly from the beginning of the 1970s, was inflationary. This is a complex argument, but can perhaps be put as follows (inflation is discussed more fully in the next chapter).

The object of demand management is to maintain full employment. If, as was broadly speaking the case in Britain during the post-war decades, average output per man in the economy rises by about $2\frac{1}{2}$ per cent a year and the labour force by $\frac{1}{2}$ per cent, then output (the GDP, in real terms) must rise by 3 per cent a year if there is to be no change in unemployment. If the inflation rate is zero, there is no problem: the GDP will have to rise by 3 per cent in *money* terms as well as in *real* terms.

Now suppose that, because of increases in wages or import prices which have already taken place, the Treasury's forecasts indicate that over the next year the inflation rate will not be zero but, say, 2 per cent. If the GDP in *real* terms is to rise by 3 per cent, then clearly – since prices are going to rise by 2 per cent – the GDP in *money* terms must rise by 5 per cent. So the government must use its fiscal and monetary instruments to secure a 5 per cent increase in effective demand, in money terms; and this can easily be seen as validating and even encouraging inflation.

The problem can be seen at its most acute in the case of the government's own expenditure, at a time when factors entirely outside the government's control – like the 1973–4 oil shock – cause inflation to be higher than allowed for in the forecasts. If (to oversimplify by ignoring the obvious measurement problems in this sector) the government wants the 'output' of, for example, the health service to rise by 3 per cent, and forecasts that the relevant price indices will rise by 2 per cent, it will make available 5 per cent more money. Suppose, however, that as the year wears on it becomes apparent that prices are going to be not 2 per cent higher but 4 per cent higher. The logic of demand management requires the government to make available a further 2 per cent more money to cover these higher prices since, if it does not, the output of the health sector will rise by less than the planned 3 per cent, and some of those employed in the sector will lose their jobs. But if the government does make this further 2 per cent more money available, it will not only be validating inflation but inviting faster inflation in the future, because managers in the health service will have no incentive to minimize costs or resist excessive wage or salary claims: they will be permitted to employ the same number of doctors and nurses as originally planned, regardless of what they cost.

This kind of problem was resolved, after a fashion, by the introduction in 1976 of 'cash limits' on government expenditure. A government department or agency would now be given a certain amount of cash each year on the basis of a particular inflation forecast. If inflation turned out to be higher than that, well, that was just too bad. (Clearly, this replaced the risk of encouraging inflation by the risk – some would say the certainty – of underfunding many public services.)

The two criticisms of demand management discussed so far have a certain validity. Nevertheless, it can be argued that they represent a case against the way it was conducted at certain times rather than a case against demand management as such. Yes, it may be conceded, under Barber the time-lags in the system were underestimated: too much demand was injected into the economy too quickly, and the consequence was an accelerating rate of inflation. Yes, some post-war governments were too ready to see macroeconomic policy purely in terms of influencing *real* variables (output and employment), relying excessively on other instruments – notably prices and incomes policies – to keep the inflation rate low. These instruments were not powerful enough to offset the inflationary pressures sometimes associated with the attempt to keep the *volume* of output growing at a particular rate regardless of prevailing circumstances. Nevertheless, both these types of error could be rectified without abandoning the practice of demand management.

The third criticism of demand management was the one advanced by Milton Friedman and the monetarists, and was much more basic. According to this school of thought, demand management was fundamentally misconceived, and bound to lead to accelerating inflation. It was this analysis in particular that underlay the macroeconomic policy – or lack of it – pursued in Britain from 1979 onwards.

The argument, in general, was based on the same assumptions as those made by economists in the nineteenth century: the economy was fundamentally stable and needed no intervention, at the macro level, by the government. What this analysis meant, in practice, was that the government should balance its own budget and control the growth of the money supply. Market forces would do the rest, bringing about a fully employed economy, with zero inflation, growing at the rate permitted by the underlying increase in productivity and the labour force. Some of the reasons why the monetarists expected this happy outcome of an absence of government intervention were the same as those advanced by the classical economists. But the monetarists added a few features of their own. Briefly, their version proceeds as follows.

If the government confines itself to balancing the budget and controlling the money supply, the economy and the various markets that compose it – financial markets, goods markets, the labour market, etc. – will settle down into an equilibrium. Particularly important, in the context of the present argument, is the labour market. Here wage rates, and the level of employment, are simultaneously determined by supply and demand. The presumption is that at high wage rates plenty of people will want to work, but employers will not want to employ many of them: it is no good employing someone at a wage greater than the value of what he produces. At low wages, correspondingly, employers will want to employ plenty of people, but not too many people will be willing to work. The equilibrium level of employment will be established somewhere between high wages and low wages, at that precise wage at which the number of people who want to work is equal to the number of people whom employers will want to employ. This level of employment is, implicitly, full employment, though the monetarists put the point somewhat differently. Any unemployment that exists when the economy has reached this equilibrium, they say, represents *the natural rate of unemployment* for the economy concerned.

The natural rate, according to the monetarists, represents unemployment that is *voluntary*. It is the result of a deliberate decision, on the part of workers, not to work at the wage rate established by market forces. If they were willing to work at this wage, they would not be unemployed. But, for whatever mixture of reasons, they choose not to work. So they are not really unemployed at all, according to this analysis: there is, in effect, full employment.

Just as market forces lead in this way to 'full employment', so they also lead to stable prices. Employers will increase wages only if the value of a worker's output increases. If on average (to take the figure used earlier) this increases by 2½ per cent a year, then wages will increase by 2½ per cent a year, but by definition this will not lead to any increase in prices because higher wages are being financed out of higher productivity.

So there we have it: Nirvana. By doing nothing but balancing the budget and controlling the money supply, the government has created a situation in which the economy grows, prices are stable and any unemployment represents the exercise of individual choice.

The reason why demand management is bound to be inflationary, according to this story, is that for most of the time it represents an attempt to keep unemployment below its natural rate. And when unemployment is below its natural rate, inflation will be accelerating (just as, for symmetry, when unemployment is above the natural rate, inflation will be decelerating). Only at the natural rate of unemployment will inflation be stable. Whether it will be stable at zero, or 2 per cent, or 5 per cent will depend on past history; the point is that it will not accelerate. For simplicity of exposition, we assume in the next few paragraphs that at the natural rate of unemployment the inflation rate is initially stable at zero – i.e. there is no change, over time, in the price level.

The inflation rate accelerates when unemployment is pushed down below its natural rate, according to this account, because a divergence develops between the actual inflation rate and the expected inflation rate. This is a story that can become quite complicated. Perhaps it does not represent too much of a caricature of the monetarist version of events to put it as follows.

Unemployment, let us suppose, is initially at its natural rate, but the government, in its ignorance, decides that this level of unemployment is too high: it does not represent what it regards as 'full employment'. It therefore takes steps to increase effective demand. These may take the form of an expansionary fiscal policy (tax cuts or increases in public expenditure, creating or increasing a budget deficit) or an expansionary monetary policy (lower interest rates and an increase in the money supply). Whatever form these measures take, the result will be an increase in effective demand in the economy – i.e. in the actual expenditure of households (on consumer goods), businesses (on investment goods) or the government itself. Faced by an increase in the demand for their products, employers will find it profitable to take on more labour, and in order to do this they will have to offer higher wages (since everyone who wants to work at the existing wage rate is already doing so).

The scene now shifts to a pub, at 11 o'clock on a Monday morning, where Bill and Ben (the rational men) are sitting studying the racing form in the tabloids. Some time ago Bill and Ben took careful note of the wage they would get if they took a job and decided that it wasn't worth it. They are, therefore, voluntarily unemployed (part of the natural rate of unemployment), and the beer and small cigars they are enjoying are accordingly financed by the social security benefits they receive from an indulgent state (though other, unspecified, sources of income have also been rumoured). Suddenly Bill's eye is caught by a job advertisement. Employers are offering 3 per cent more than they were last week! At this wage it *is* worth getting a job. Ben agrees. Off they go to the Jobcentre. They take jobs. Unemployment falls.

A year passes. Bill and Ben are back in the pub, but it is evening, because they work during the day. Bill has noticed something extremely disconcerting. Prices have risen by 3 per cent. (Prices have risen by 3 per cent because the increase in effective demand, and thus in output and employment, has not led to any increases in productivity, or output *per man*, and in order to maintain their profit margins employers have had to pass on higher wages, and other costs, in higher prices.) This 3 per cent price increase has cancelled out the 3 per cent wage increase that induced Bill and Ben to take a job. There has been no increase in the *real* wage at all. They were lured back to work by a false prospectus. They have been conned. They were not willing to work for this real wage before, and they are not willing to now. Next morning finds them back in the pub. They have packed in their jobs and are once again voluntarily unemployed. Unemployment, which had been artificially reduced by selling workers a false bill of goods, rises back to the natural rate.

But although unemployment goes back to what it was, inflation does not. Previously, the inflation rate was zero, and everybody expected it to continue at zero, and behaved accordingly, and so it stayed at zero. Now the inflation rate is 3 per cent, and everybody expects it to continue at 3 per cent, and behaves accordingly, and so it stays at 3 per cent. There has been a once-for-all increase in inflation, from a stable rate of zero to a stable rate of 3 per cent a year. This might not matter too much, it could be argued, if the government had learned its lesson and never again tried to drive unemployment down below the natural rate. But it has not learned its lesson, or will soon forget it. Before long the whole sorry saga will be repeated, and inflation will rise to 6 per cent. And then to 9 per cent. And so on.

The implication of this monetarist analysis is that unemployment cannot be reduced by Keynesian demand management, except temporarily and damagingly. To put it another way: only in the very short run can *real* variables, such as output and employment, be affected by demand management. This does not mean that unemployment cannot be reduced. It can: but only by reducing the natural rate of unemployment itself. Some of the ways in which this can be done would – or should – be applauded by everyone, not just monetarists: more training and retraining is an obvious example, since it helps to match the skills of the unemployed with the vacancies that are unfilled. Others, such as measures to reduce the bargaining power of trade unions, and thus their ability to secure inflationary wage increases, might command wide agreement as well. But many of the measures advocated by the monetarists to reduce the natural rate of unemployment depend on the validity of the monetarist analysis: they are designed to make it less appealing to be voluntarily unemployed. They include a reduction in unemployment benefits by cutting them directly, or taxing them, or not indexing them to inflation, or withdrawing them altogether after a short time; and, in general, making it much more uncomfortable, for both a worker and his family, if he decides to stay unemployed. Bill and Ben will be able to afford only the occasional half pint and own-rolled cigarette, and will not be any too popular at home.

This monetarist critique of demand management, and in particular its explanation of how demand management inevitably generates inflation, was seized on eagerly by Mrs Thatcher in the mid-1970s, and became the driving force behind her economic policies after she formed a government in 1979. It had the advantage of killing two birds with one stone.

First, it identified the cause of inflation and provided a very simple remedy for it: balance the budget and control the money supply. But because initially (in 1979–80) the inflation rate was too high, there would have to be a transitional period during which unemployment was kept *above* the natural rate, so that the inflation rate would fall. When it had fallen to a satisfactory level, unemployment would come down to its natural rate, and provided that the budget continued to be balanced and the money supply kept under control, a low and stable rate of inflation would be secured for the indefinite future.

The second advantage of the monetarist critique, which it would be naïve to overlook, is that it legitimized some of the more basic instincts of Mrs Thatcher and her supporters on the Conservative right. By the 1970s, in their view, the country had well and truly gone to the dogs: a sad decline from some golden age seventy-five or 100 years earlier (Mrs Thatcher was a great one for 'Victorian values', without actually seeming to know much about what they were). The workers did not work properly any more. Why should they? Social security benefits were generous; education was free; health care was free; council housing was heavily subsidized, as was public transport. And so on. No wonder the pubs and betting shops were full of welfare scroungers. To the ears of Mrs Thatcher and much of her Cabinet (virtually all of her Cabinet, after she had conducted a series of purges) the monetarist message could not fail to be the sweetest of music.

This does not, however, alter the fact that the message is nonsense. No doubt there is a Bill here and a Ben there; but most of the unemployment Britain has suffered in the 1980s and early 1990s has been *involuntary* – a simple consequence of too low a level of effective demand in the economy. More generally, what is wrong with monetarism is what was wrong with the classical economics that Keynes criticized in the 1930s. It is a theory that is based on wholly unrealistic assumptions. The economy is not self-stabilizing at full employment. No unique equilibrium is automatically created by the operation of market forces, at which all of the economy's resources are fully utilized. And it is not even the case that when some sudden shock impinges on the economy, shoving it away from this equilibrium, the operation of market forces will quickly and painlessly redeploy resources away from old uses and into new ones, restoring equilibrium at full employment. There was some justification for these assumptions in the late eighteenth and early nineteenth centuries, when the foundations of classical economics were laid down, because at that time firms were small in relation to the size of the market, unions in their infancy, real wages low and social security benefits non-existent. Workers who lost their jobs had to redeploy themselves fast or starve (and even this feature of the nineteenth-century economy, which some monetarist economists and politicians appear to view with nostalgia, did not prevent prolonged recessions). But there was much less reason to cling to such assumptions in the early decades of the twentieth century, when these conditions had largely disappeared, let alone resurrect them towards the end of it.

The fact is that the economy, if left unmanaged, does not settle down at an equilibrium at which unemployment is at the natural rate, and the inflation rate is stable. It may settle at a low unemployment equilibrium, or a high unemployment equilibrium, or at no equilibrium at all: it all depends on the level of effective demand, in relation to the productive capacity of the economy, and what is happening to it. Nor does the notion of a unique link between the rate of unemployment and the rate of inflation make much sense. It is easy to see that if unemployment is high, there is likely to be less inflation than if it is low; also that if unemployment is *rising*, inflation is likely to be less of a problem than if unemployment is *falling*. But to move from this common-sense insight to the assertion that there is one unique rate of unemployment at which the inflation rate will be stable is to suppose that the economy behaves like some kind of machine, and to apply to it concepts more appropriate to the engineering laboratory. The inflation rate over any given period of time is determined by a variety of factors, of which the unemployment rate is only one.

The concept of the natural rate of unemployment, it might be added, would carry more conviction if monetarists could put a figure on it, and stick to it. Then at least we would all know what rate of unemployment we have to put up with in order to enjoy a stable rate of inflation. But such figures have been hard to come by, and when they have been forthcoming they have not helped much. In a book published in 1983 a leading British monetarist, Patrick Minford, put the natural rate of unemployment a decade or so earlier, in 1971, at 1 million, or about 5 per cent. A second edition of the book, published two years later, suggested it had been 2.4 million, or about 12 per cent. The figure for the natural rate of unemployment in 1980 differed between the two editions, too: at first it was put at 8–10 per cent, then at about $13\frac{1}{2}$ per cent. Moreover, the early 1970s witnessed the spectacle, embarrassing for monetarist theory, of inflation rising rapidly at a time when unemployment was also rising rapidly. Nothing daunted, the monetarists came up with a neat explanation of this unscheduled phenomenon. Although actual unemployment was rising rapidly, they said, the natural rate of unemployment was also – for mysterious reasons – rising rapidly, so the actual rate of unemployment was still below the natural rate; hence, of course, inflation was rising. Such ingenuity, one feels, was worthy of a better cause.

Nonsense though it is, the monetarist doctrine that the economy is self-stabilizing at full employment, and government intervention not just unnecessary, but harmful, has had a pervasive effect on economic policy for a decade and a half. It started to influence policymaking in Britain in the mid-1970s, and came into its own with a vengeance when Mrs Thatcher's government took office in 1979. It was still, albeit in somewhat modified form, the main intellectual basis of policy in the early 1990s. Only in the autumn of 1992 were some elements of it jettisoned, and then only under the pressure of events (including the forced withdrawal of sterling from the ERM, and dissension in the Tory ranks over the Maastricht Treaty) that threatened the government's survival. It was not immediately clear whether the junkie had really kicked the habit or had merely suppressed it until the heat was off.

3

INFLATION: FASHIONABLE STAGE VILLAIN

For most of the past couple of decades inflation has been the villain of the economic piece. Like Captain Hook in *Peter Pan*, its appearance on the stage was always sure to be greeted with a chorus of boos and hisses. Mrs Thatcher put its defeat at the top of her agenda. Mr Lawson said that the inflation rate would be 'judge and jury' of his monetary policy. His two successors as Chancellor concurred. Since a great deal (of which more later) has clearly been sacrificed over the past couple of decades in the battle against inflation, it may be useful to examine exactly what inflation is and why it is regarded as so noxious.

As everyone knows, inflation means rising prices; but a slightly more rigorous definition would be something like 'a sustained rise, over time, in the price of a representative collection of the goods and services consumed by a typical household'. This definition stresses that inflation is a concept that applies not to *particular* prices but to the *average* price of goods and services. The prices of individual goods and services can move against the average, depending on such factors as the scope for technological progress and the extent to which the product or service is labour-intensive. Electronic calculators and long-distance telephone calls are actually cheaper than they were twenty years ago. Theatre tickets and restaurant meals, on the other hand, cost ten or fifteen times as much. The inflation rate is an average of all these price changes, weighted according to people's expenditure on different items. The best-known inflation indicator in Britain is the *retail price index*, which measures what has happened each month to the price of a basket of goods and services bought by the average household. The retail price index is now about six times what it was twenty years ago – an average inflation rate over the period of about $9\frac{1}{2}$ per cent. (During the fourteen years since Mrs Thatcher took office the inflation rate has averaged about 7 per cent).

34

The inflation rate has been positive – i.e. the retail price index has risen – every year since 1935. So inflation has been with us for a long time. Taking a loftier historical perspective, however, it is a relatively recent phenomenon. There is, of course, something rather unreal about attempts to assess what has happened to the price of a representative basket of goods over a period of several centuries (there were no electronic calculators or telephone calls in 1600, though there were undoubtedly theatre tickets and restaurant meals). Nevertheless, heroic attempts have been made. The price level in 1900 seems to have been less than double what it had been three centuries earlier – an almost infinitesimally small average annual inflation rate; and prices were actually lower in 1900 than they had been in 1800.

Whether the twentieth century has been better than the nineteenth, or worse, is an excellent subject for school debating societies; but even if the conclusion is that it has been worse, it is not obvious that the reason has much to do with the two centuries' experience of inflation. Nevertheless, inflation is generally regarded as a very bad thing, and it is necessary to look in some detail at just why this is.

It seems appropriate to start with an argument sometimes advanced by the Conservative government in the early 1990s in support of the intention it then frequently proclaimed, to reduce inflation to zero. This argument is that inflation *causes* unemployment.

This is a curious argument. It implies that low unemployment is the *real* objective of the government's policy, and that zero inflation is being pursued simply in order to attain this end. But if low unemployment is really the objective, why not target it directly? There is an *Alice in Wonderland* logic to the notion that the way to achieve low unemployment is to pursue policies that raise unemployment from 5 or 6 per cent to 10 or 12 per cent – and have done so twice in a decade.

But perhaps the argument is a bit more sophisticated. It might, if reduced to the simplest possible terms, be illustrated like this. Suppose that the GDP (or total output of the economy) is £100 – i.e. the total volume or quantity of output (Q) times its average price (P) is equal to £100. If, to take an optimistic view, increases in productivity, or output per man, make it possible, with no change in employment, for the volume of output to rise by 3 per cent a year, and if there is a zero inflation rate (unchanged average prices), then GDP, or PQ, can rise by 3 per cent a year. Thus, as the years go by, PQ will be £100, £103, £106.09, £109.27, etc., all of these rises being accounted for by the rising volume of output, since the price level is stable. And because the volume of output is rising at the rate made possible by increases in productivity, by definition employment and unemployment will be unchanged.

Equipped with this simple model, it is possible to see what might be meant by the assertion 'inflation *causes* unemployment'. If the government is determined to maintain a stable price level, the GDP, or PQ, cannot be permitted to rise by more than 3 per cent a year because that is the limit made possible by the growth of productivity. But if the government succeeds in keeping PQ rising by 3 per cent a year and there is in fact some rise in the price level, then Q must rise by less than 3 per cent. If the price level rises by 2 per cent a year, for example, then Q will rise by only 1 per cent. And – given the assumption about rising productivity – if Q rises by only 1 per cent, it follows that employment must fall and unemployment must rise. That, then, is the sense in which it is true that 'inflation causes unemployment'.

But the reason why inflation has caused unemployment is not that we are the helpless victims of some physical law inherent in the way the universe is constructed. The reason is that the government has prevented PQ from rising by more than 3 per cent (or, in the slightly emotive language sometimes used, has refused to 'accommodate' inflation). Of this one may approve or disapprove, but it is not something beyond human control. It simply represents the government's set of priorities. So the assertion that 'inflation causes unemployment' might be more honestly restated as 'if there is a choice between tolerating inflation and tolerating unemployment, we are going to tolerate unemployment'.

That said, the spurious nature of the argument that inflation causes unemployment does not necessarily mean that inflation is a tolerable state of affairs. Some of the genuine arguments against inflation must now be discussed.

First of all, inflation is unpopular, and in a democracy governments have to pay some attention to this (though not always all that much, to judge by how long it took the 1987–92 Conservative government to admit it had been wrong about the poll tax). The reasons for the unpopularity of inflation, however, are not all well grounded. Human nature is more inclined to notice prices which have gone up than prices which have come down, and people would still be complaining about rising prices even if the retail price index were flat.

More significant is an aspect of what has been called 'money illusion' – though this illusion is probably much less pronounced now than it was thirty or forty years ago. It is a tendency to assume that changes in *money* variables are the same thing as changes in *real* variables. If – to go back to the earlier example – a country's overall productivity, or output per man, is rising by 3 per cent a year, then (ignoring changes in the size of the labour force, the terms of trade with other countries, etc.) average living standards, or *real* incomes, can rise by 3 per cent a year. This would happen if money incomes (or GDP, or PQ) rose by 3 per cent a year and prices were stable. But it would also happen if money incomes (or GDP, or PQ) rose by 7 per cent a year, and prices by 4 per cent. People might complain about the 4 per cent inflation rate without taking due account of the fact that their money incomes were rising by 7 per cent. They would prefer – they say – zero inflation, without realizing that in that case their money incomes would be rising by only 3 per cent a year. In other words, what determines the growth in their real incomes is the growth in the average productivity of the economy, and this has very little to do with what is happening to prices or to *money* incomes.

Although this argument may apply to the economy as a whole, or to people on average, it does not necessarily apply to everybody. If somebody's income is fixed in money terms, it will make a lot of difference to him or her whether inflation is zero, or 4 per cent, or 25 per cent. Absolutely fixed incomes are, in fact, a rarity nowadays because after more than half a century of inflation institutional arrangements have accommodated themselves to it. Most public-sector pensions, for example, are explicitly linked to the retail price index, and much the same applies *de facto* in the private sector. State benefits, too, are regularly upgraded in line with inflation. Nevertheless, some incomes are more fixed than others, and there must be a presumption that some people do worse under a moderately high inflation rate than they would under a lower, or zero, one. But whether this matters perhaps depends on who they are, whether they are rich or poor, worthy or unworthy; and this takes us into deeper philosophical waters than can be embarked on here. The basic point is that although the effects on the distribution of *real* incomes of a 4 per cent inflation rate will be different, in complex ways, from the effects of a zero inflation rate, it is not self-evident that they will be worse. So this objection to inflation is not particularly persuasive.

A more powerful argument against inflation concerns the balance of payments. In a regime of fixed exchange rates, in which countries are required to maintain the value of their currencies within very narrow limits in terms of other currencies, problems can arise if different countries have different inflation rates. Countries with relatively high inflation rates will find their goods and services becoming less competitive in both home and export markets, and will move into increasing deficit on their balance of payments (on current account). Correspondingly, countries with relatively low inflation rates will move into increasing balance-of-payments surpluses (most governments would prefer a surplus to a deficit, but surpluses, too, can pose problems).

This state of affairs would not matter too much if governments made timely adjustments to the rate at which their currency is pegged to other currencies – i.e. revalued or devalued – to offset the effects of the different inflation rates. But for a variety of reasons they are usually reluctant to do this. One good reason is that if countries are going to change their exchange rates whenever things start to get difficult, the fixed exchange-rate regime soon becomes a fiction, and the reality, for better or worse, becomes some kind of floating exchange-rate regime. A related argument is the 'discipline' argument (often heard from those who had a public-school education). This is that a fixed exchange-rate regime exerts a necessary discipline on inflation-prone countries precisely because of the unpleasant consequences of having a higher inflation rate than other countries; and obviously this will not work if the necessary discipline can be neatly avoided by devaluing from one fixed exchange rate to another.

Although these arguments have some force, uncritical accept-ance of them can entail real dangers. Take a country that – for whatever historical, cultural or other reasons – has a relatively high inflation rate and consequently (under a fixed exchange-rate regime) a deteriorating balance of payments. If it resists devaluation, it is likely to be forced into deflationary measures. Taxes will have to be increased, or public expenditure cut, or interest rates raised. These measures will help to reduce the balance-of-payments deficit by reducing incomes and output, and hence the size of the import bill. In the case of higher interest rates they will also help to *finance* the balance-of-pay-ments deficit by encouraging foreigners to buy the country's currency now that the higher rate of return they can get on it offsets the risk that at some point in the future it may, after all, have to be devalued.

The danger is that such deflationary measures will not have nearly enough effect in reducing inflation to restore the balance of payments to a viable position at the existing exchange rate. All that will happen is that the inevitable devaluation is post-poned. And in the meantime incomes and output fall, and unemployment rises. This is precisely what happened as a result of the Labour government's stubborn refusal to devalue what was clearly an overvalued pound in 1964 (devaluation did not come until November 1967); and it is precisely what happened as the result of the Conservative government's entry into the European Exchange Rate Mechanism in October 1990 at what was clearly an overvalued exchange rate, and its subsequent blinkered refusal, for almost two years, to accept the necessary realignment (see chapter 4).

If it is in a fixed exchange-rate regime, it might therefore be concluded, things will be easier all round if a country has an inflation rate that is about the same as other countries' – whether this be zero, 2 per cent, 4 per cent or whatever. Nevertheless, if it has a somewhat higher inflation rate, that is not the end of the world. The ensuing balance-of-payments difficulties, or pressure on the currency, should be dealt with not by a savage deflation that reduces output, cuts investment, raises unemployment and generally throws the baby out with the bath water, but by a timely and judicious realignment of exchange rates. (Of course, if this cannot be done because the currency is irrevocably fixed against other currencies, as would *de facto* be the case if Europe came to have a single currency, the baby probably will get thrown out with the bath water. This issue is taken up in chapter 7.)

So far, at least, the usual arguments for the assertion that inflation is an evil that must be eliminated, and that a zero or very low inflation rate must be an overriding aim of government policy, do not emerge very convincingly from close examination. But there is one final argument. This is that once inflation comes to be tolerated, it will not obligingly stay at some modest level but will accelerate; that accelerating inflation will lead to hyper-inflation; and that hyper-inflation is a disaster to be avoided at all costs.

With the last of these propositions it is difficult to disagree. It is well known that the hyper-inflation of 1923 destroyed the German middle classes and paved the way for the arrival of Hitler. A state of affairs in which prices double between breakfast and lunch, and double again before dinnertime, is an unsustainable one: before long no one is getting much in the way of meals of any kind. Inflation on this scale always ends in some kind of smash-up. Even accelerating inflation on a far more modest scale can be frightening. It was observed in chapter 1 that inflation in Britain accelerated from 6 per cent in 1970 to over 25 per cent in 1975. It was, in fact, reduced sharply in 1976 and subsequent years, and was back below 10 per cent by 1979. But what if it had been 50 per cent in 1976 and 150 per cent in 1977?

The nation would not have been facing the abyss; it would have been well and truly into it.

The question is not, however, whether accelerating inflation can lead to disaster; clearly it can. The question is why should an inflation rate of, say, 4 or 5 per cent be more likely to accelerate than an inflation rate of 2 per cent or zero? And the answer is far from clear.

The ultimate cause of inflation is to be found among the seven deadly sins, avarice and envy being perhaps the most relevant. In a market economy, if people collectively want more goods and services than the economy is capable of producing, then prices will rise. (In a centrally planned economy, like that of the former Soviet Union, where prices are controlled, shortages and queues will develop.) This is not necessarily because, in the popular phrase, 'too much money is chasing too few goods'. Inflation may be mainly of this 'demand–pull' variety, but it may be more of the 'cost–push' variety, in which powerful groups of workers succeed in winning large wage increases, which firms then pass on in price increases (which may, in turn, fuel further large wage increases). This can happen even when there is not, in the conventional sense, any excess demand in the economy at all. Whichever of these features predominates, however, the fact is that the totality of individual demands on the real resources of the economy exceeds the quantity of the real resources available, and prices rise to reconcile the two.

This being so, there is always a danger that inflation will accelerate. A very simple example can illustrate the point. Suppose that people want a 5 per cent rise in their real income, or standard of living, and – on the assumption that prices will remain stable – succeed in negotiating a 5 per cent rise in their wages and salaries. If, as in earlier examples, the total output of the economy can grow by only 3 per cent a year, prices will rise by 2 per cent to eliminate the difference. But then, of course, *real* incomes will only have risen by 3 per cent (the 5 per cent rise in money incomes minus the 2 per cent rise in prices). Aha! people say to themselves: with prices rising by 2 per cent a year, to get a rise in our living standards of 5 per cent we obviously need a wage increase of 7 per cent. And, of course, if they get it, prices next year will rise by 4 per cent in order to eliminate the difference. And so on. In short, inflation accelerates.

However, although this example demonstrates how inflation can accelerate, it does not demonstrate why this should be more likely to happen if the initial inflation rate is 4 or 5 per cent than if, as in this example, it is zero. And indeed it is difficult to see how any such demonstration could be provided. If the forces making for accelerating inflation are in place, inflation will accelerate even if in Year 1 it is zero. If they are not in place, then it will not accelerate even if in Year 1 it is 4 per cent.

That is the logic of the argument. Of course, if it were the case that in the real world inflation of zero per cent rarely or never accelerated, while inflation of 4 per cent usually or always did, then one would have to concede that there was something wrong with the logic. But that is not what experience suggests. There have been positive inflation rates in all advanced industrial countries in virtually every year for the past half century or more. Sometimes these rates have accelerated; sometimes they have decelerated; sometimes they have stayed the same. In Britain, as was discussed earlier, the inflation rate was fairly stable between 1945 and 1970, and since then has sometimes risen, sometimes fallen and sometimes stayed the same. Thus it is flying in the face not only of the logic but also of the facts to argue that an inflation rate of zero or 2 per cent protects against the danger of accelerating inflation in a way that an inflation rate of 4 or 5 per cent does not.

So far, this chapter has been concerned with the question of what good reasons there might be for a government to make the achievement of zero inflation the main, or indeed the only, goal of its economic policy. And the conclusion has been that such reasons are hard to find. Not even the virtues of a positive but very low rate of inflation, of 1 or 2 per cent, are self-evident.

One could perhaps go on to the offensive, and ask whether there might not be some actual advantages in a moderate rate of inflation of perhaps 3 or 4 per cent a year. Certainly it has been argued in the past that a gently rising price level is good for economic growth. This is mainly because it favours debtors, including entrepreneurs who borrow money to expand or set up their businesses, at the expense of creditors – people who already possess money and just passively lend it out. Another way of putting the same point is that an economy is more likely to grow if real interest rates are low than if they are high, and real interest rates will tend to be lower if there is a moderate inflation rate than if inflation is zero or very low. This argument is a complex one, and depends on divergences between anticipated and actual inflation rates. It should not be overdone, but nor should it be dismissed out of hand.

A second reason can be put forward for supposing that there may be some virtue in a moderate rate of inflation. It helps to facilitate changes in *relative* wages (and perhaps prices) which improve economic efficiency. It is easier for some wages to rise faster than others if average earnings are rising by 7 per cent a year (and there is a 4 per cent inflation rate) than if average earnings are rising by only 3 per cent a year (and there is no inflation). This is one aspect of a more general argument – that a moderate rate of inflation may be a less damaging way than any other of resolving some of society's tensions. Intractable disputes between government and powerful interest groups, or employers and unions, or simply between different groups of workers, can sometimes be settled only if more money is produced from somewhere; and one way or another this is likely to raise the price level. In an ideal world it would not be so: employers would be reasonable; workers would be realistic; governments would stand firm. But democracy is a messy business, politics is the art of the possible, and a bit of fudging and mudging that increases a wage here and a price there may sometimes prevent a political disaster.

It might reasonably be concluded, on the basis of the arguments put forward so far in this chapter, that, *other things being equal*, a zero or exceedingly low rate of inflation is quite desirable, but is not particularly important, and may possibly be in some ways less desirable than some slightly higher rate of inflation. Other things may not, however, be equal. Nothing has been said so far about the costs of achieving and maintaining a zero or very low rate of inflation. If the costs are significant, compared with tolerating a somewhat higher rate of inflation, then the game may not be worth the candle.

In a completely rational world, there would be no costs involved in achieving a zero inflation rate. Everybody would understand that rising living standards (rising *real* incomes) depend on what happens to productivity, or real output per man, not on what happens to *money* incomes. If the productivity of the economy is rising by 3 per cent a year because of investment in new technologies, research and development, an increasingly highly trained and educated labour force, etc., then zero inflation will be consistent with a rise in average money incomes of 3 per cent a year. Of course, the efficient working of the economy would require some incomes to rise by more than 3 per cent and others by less, but in a completely rational world some mechanism would be devised to arrange for this to happen through amicable agreement rather than through strikes or other kinds of industrial action, which lead to loss of output.

Brave attempts have been made from time to time to bring this ideal state of affairs about. This was the objective of the various prices and incomes policies that were sooner or later resorted to by every post-war British government – until the arrival of Mrs Thatcher. The aim of all these policies was to get average money incomes rising by not too much more than the average rise in productivity in the economy, so as to yield a very low and stable rate of inflation. It has become fashionable nowadays to claim that incomes policies never work, always break down, etc., etc.; and indeed the problem of getting agreement on which incomes are to rise more than the average, and which more slowly, has always in the end proved an intractable one. But the efficacy of some of these policies should not be underestimated: as was noted earlier, it was the Labour government's prices and incomes policy, rather than the application of monetarist ideas, that brought the inflation rate down from more than 25 per cent in 1975 to less than 10 per cent in 1979.

However, although this and other incomes policies had more success than they are sometimes given credit for, they were not costless. They must have had some adverse effects on the efficient allocation of resources and on increases in productivity, because employers in high-growth sectors could not offer more pay in order to attract skilled labour. But these costs must be kept in perspective. If trying to achieve a very low rate of inflation by means of an incomes policy has costs in terms of resources misallocated, what about the costs of trying to achieve the same result by the policies pursued in the early 1980s and early 1990s? As was argued in chapter 1, the big fall in the inflation rate during the first half of the 1980s was accompanied by, and largely caused by, a big rise in unemployment, and exactly the same is happening again in the first half of the 1990s. There is room for argument about the amount of output lost for ever by these two recessions, but it was probably equivalent to well over a third of the 1992 GDP – a total loss of perhaps £200 billion. But even more serious than this once-for-all loss was the effect on the economy's growth *potential*. The loss of manufacturing capacity and industrial skills, and the demoralization of much of the workforce, caused by the recessions of the early 1980s and early 1990s are likely to reduce Britain's sustainable growth rate for many years to come. (This issue is discussed more fully in chapter 6.)

The moral is that there are costs involved in achieving a very low rate of inflation (and, *a fortiori*, a zero rate of inflation). These costs may be heavy if it is achieved by means of an incomes policy, but are likely to be incomparably heavier if achieved by falling output and rising unemployment. This seems to be true of Britain and of other European countries such as Italy and France, where – at any rate until relatively recently – a very low rate of inflation has not been accorded top priority as an economic objective. In other countries, such as Germany, where great importance has long been attached to very low inflation, and to the kind of consensus between employers and employees needed to achieve it, severe doses of recession may not be required to keep inflation low – though recent developments in Germany suggest that this may be less true now than in the past. But different countries have different histories, preoccupations, folk-myths and social structures, and it would be naïve to suppose that the costs of securing a low inflation rate will never be any greater in one country than another.

The plain fact is that a very low inflation rate is not the only objective of economic policy. It is not even the most important objective. In a world of scarce resources and unsatisfied needs, the main objective of economic policy must be to ensure that existing resources are fully utilized – i.e. that there should be full employment. Another objective is that the amount of resources should increase over time – i.e. that there should be a reasonable rate of growth of the economy (something that requires adequate levels of investment, research, education and training).

Other objectives relate to how a growing GDP is used, or divided up. How far should expenditure decisions be taken by individuals, and how far by central or local government and financed out of tax revenues? How far should the state intervene to influence the interpersonal distribution of income, taxing the rich to alleviate the lot of the poor? All these are genuine issues, which relate in one way or another to people's living standards, in the widest sense of the term. By contrast, the question of whether the inflation rate should be zero, or 2 per cent, or 4 per cent is hardly a genuine issue at all. It relates not to real things but to mere symbols or labels. To make this question a crucial test – let alone *the* crucial test – of a successful economic policy is the sheerest folly.

The argument of this chapter can be simply summarized. A zero, or even a very low, rate of inflation is not a particularly important objective of a rational economic policy, certainly much less important than low unemployment or a reasonably high rate of growth of output. Rapidly accelerating inflation is indeed dangerous and to be avoided like the plague, but there is no obvious reason why inflation running at a moderate rate of 4 per cent is more likely to accelerate than an inflation rate of zero or 1 per cent. And in Britain, where inflation has not been as low as zero for nearly sixty years, all the evidence is that to get inflation down to zero and keep it there (except, conceivably, by some kind of incomes policy) would be horrendously costly in terms of other, real, objectives of economic policy. Inflation must be kept under control; but it must also be kept in perspective.

4

THE THATCHER EXPERIMENT:
DOGMA AND DISASTER

It was argued in chapter 2 that a modern industrial economy does not manage itself. Market forces do not operate in such a way as to stabilize it at full employment. The effective demand represented by the decisions of hundreds of thousands of businesses and tens of millions of households may just happen to be enough to generate the amount of output that will create full, but not over-full, employment; but it may not. And when it does not, it is the job of the government to increase or reduce effective demand as required. This was the policy pursued in Britain between 1941 and the late 1970s. Regular forecasts were made of the likely path of effective demand over the next year or two, and adjustments to fiscal, monetary and other policies were made as necessary. The forecasts were not perfect, nor was knowledge of exactly how the economy would react to changes in the setting of policy instruments. In the early 1970s, with the Barber boom, things certainly got out of hand. But lessons were learned from that episode. By and large, in a rough and ready way, it all worked reasonably well – certainly better than the alternative that succeeded it. However, this approach to the economy, known as demand management, began to go out of fashion in the later 1970s, and was abandoned altogether when Mrs Thatcher took office in 1979.

The shift in attitude during the 1970s, away from the idea that low unemployment was the main aim of economic policy towards the conviction that the main aim must be low inflation, was remarked on earlier (page 4). But the 1970s saw another sea change in attitudes as well: the emergence of the view that government had become too big and too interventionist; that the pursuit of consensus between government, employers and trade unions had led to an unwieldy and inefficient corporate state; and that the free operation of market forces had been

47

widely and damagingly suppressed. These views had been power-
fully articulated and promoted by Mrs Thatcher after she became
Leader of the Conservative Party in 1975, and when she arrived
in Downing Street in 1979 her pledge to 'roll back the frontiers
of the state' was every bit as emphatic as her promise to defeat
inflation. Market forces must be given their head. Public expenditure must be reduced. Taxes must be cut. Trade union privileges
and immunities must be removed. The economy must be deregu-
lated. And – because the economy was assumed to be self-
stabilizing at full employment – macroeconomic policy should
be neutral. The growth of the money supply should be kept in
line with the growth of total output, and the budget should be
balanced. That was it.

The central contention of the present book is that this approach to economic policymaking is fundamentally wrong. In
this chapter its disastrous impact on the history of the last
decade and a half is briefly traced.

The period can be broken down into three phases. The first
phase lasted from Mrs Thatcher's election victory in May 1979
until the mid-1980s and might, in the spirit of one of the most
obtrusive graffiti of the time, be described as *Money Supply
Rules OK?*. The second phase lasted from the mid-1980s until 16
September 1992 and might be characterized as *Exchange Rate
Rules OK?*. The third phase, which succeeded 16 September
1992 ('Black Wednesday'), might be entitled *Chaos Rules OK?*.
(Optimists could conceive of a footnote saying that, as with the
creation of the universe, out of chaos there might, one day,
emerge order; but there was little sign of this at the beginning of
1993.)

During the first of these phases the government concentrated
on trying to control the money supply, without worrying very
much about what happened to the exchange rate. During the
second phase it concentrated on trying to control the exchange
rate, without worrying very much about what happened to the
money supply. During the third phase it appeared to be
concentrating on everything (or – what is the same thing –
nothing). But throughout these twists and turns one thing remained constant: the idea that the economy was basically self-

regulating, and it was therefore the government's job not to seek to influence the level of effective demand, but simply to balance its own budget.

At the heart of the first phase of this sorry saga lay the Medium Term Financial Strategy (MTFS), something invented by Mr Nigel Lawson in 1979 when he was a junior minister at the Treasury. The Strategy did at least have the virtue of looking at the medium term and not just at the next year or two: it had a four-year horizon, designed to be rolled one year forward as each year elapsed. That virtue apart, however, it was fatally misconceived.

Underlying the MTFS were the two basic tenets of monetarism discussed in earlier chapters: the idea that inflation is caused by excessive growth of the money supply, and that excessive growth of the money supply is caused by government borrowing from the banking system. But, except perhaps in the long run, there is no particular relationship between the money supply and the price level – a point demonstrated empirically on page 6. (One reason for this is that the *velocity of circulation* – the number of times each pound coin, so to speak, changes hands each year – is variable.) And, in so far as there is a relationship between what happens to the money supply and what happens to the price level, many economists would argue that the direction of causality is precisely the opposite of the one assumed by the monetarists: that changes in the money supply are the effect of changes in the price level, and not the cause of them. Thus a strategy that aims to reduce the inflation rate simply by reducing the rate of increase in the money supply is unlikely to be successful.

The other assumption underlying the MTFS was equally unreal. Governments *may* finance their budget deficits by borrowing from the banking system, but there is no reason why they have to: they may finance deficits by selling government securities to the 'non-bank private sector' – insurance companies, pension funds, investment trusts, etc. This will *not* increase the money supply. (Ninety-eight per cent of government borrowing during the last three years of the 1970s did, in fact, take this form, so that over this period the contribution of budget deficits to the growth of the money supply was virtually zero.) Conversely, when there are large increases in the money supply, this is often not because the government is borrowing to finance its deficit, but because businesses and households are borrowing to finance theirs. This is exactly what happened when deregulation of the financial system led to the great credit boom of the later 1980s.

Quite apart from the extreme intellectual flimsiness of the argument that budget deficits increase the money supply and that increases in the money supply cause inflation, the attempt to rein back the growth of the money supply in the early 1980s proved wholly unsuccessful. During the first three years of the decade, for example, the government's preferred measure of the money supply, 'sterling M3', rose by about 50 per cent – twice as much as was laid down in the MTFS. (There is a point here for the connoisseur of incompetence in high places. Sterling M3 is a broad definition of the money supply, which includes interest-bearing bank deposits. The very high short-term rates of interest that the government maintained in the early 1980s – Minimum Lending Rate was at 17 per cent from November 1979 until July 1980, for example – in its attempts to control the money supply meant that it was often profitable for people to sell long-term securities and put the money on deposit. Thus there was a tendency for higher interest rates to lead to an increase in the particular measure of the money supply the government was concerned with, which in turn prompted the government to raise interest rates even further. Interestingly, this absurd vicious circle was replicated a decade later, not in Britain but by the supposedly infallible Bundesbank in Germany. It, too, focused on a broad definition of the money supply, which included interest-bearing bank deposits, and proceeded to raise interest rates to damaging levels, and to keep them there, in a self-defeating attempt to slow down the growth of its chosen monetary measure. Some of the effects of this perverse behaviour of the Bundesbank are examined in chapter 7.)

The very high interest rates maintained by the government in its futile and pointless struggle to control the money supply, as prescribed in the MTFS, were the last thing Britain needed in the early 1980s. The world economy was sliding into recession, mainly because of the deflationary effects of the second oil shock (oil prices had doubled between early 1979 and early 1980). Not only did high interest rates have a directly depressing effect on investment; they also attracted into London a lot of 'hot money' – money that came in simply to take advantage of high short-term interest rates and could go out again at any moment. This inflow of hot money pushed up the exchange rate, which was floating freely, since during this early phase of post-1979 history the government's undiluted faith in the virtues of market forces applied to the exchange rate as to nearly everything else. The rise in the value of sterling was further boosted by the fact that North Sea oil was now being pumped out at a rapid rate. This not only had a beneficial, if strictly temporary, effect on Britain's balance of payments; it also turned sterling into what some slick City wordsmith dubbed a 'petrocurrency' – a good currency to be in at a time when oil was selling for $35 a barrel.

All this led to a severe overvaluation of sterling. Between early 1979 and early 1981 the pound rose by 14 per cent against the dollar and almost 30 per cent against the Deutschemark. On average (taking the 'effective', or trade-weighted, exchange rate) it rose by 23 per cent. But the rise in the *real* effective exchange rate was higher than 23 per cent – over 30 per cent – because inflation in Britain over this period was significantly higher than in most other industrial countries. This made it very difficult for British manufacturing industry to compete, either at home or abroad. Between 1979 and 1981 manufacturing output fell by 15 per cent and manufacturing investment by nearly a third; it was 1988 before manufacturing investment even regained the level at which it had been in 1979. The damage done to manufacturing industry by government policy in the early 1980s marked the beginning of a process of deindustrialization in the British economy that was to be savagely aggravated by other government policies, particularly those pursued in the early 1990s.

It was not only the monetary side of the MTFS which had, directly and indirectly, a depressing effect on the economy at a time when deflationary forces were gathering strength around the world anyway. On the fiscal side policy was just as unfortunate.

The fiscal part of the MTFS called for a reduction in the PSBR (Public Sector Borrowing Requirement, or budget deficit) from around 6 per cent of the GDP in 1979–80 to around 1 per cent in 1983–4. (Most of this was to be achieved by cutting public expenditure, which was to fall by 4 per cent, in real terms.) In other words, at the end of the four-year period the budget was to be more or less balanced and was then to remain so. This is, of course, the basic monetarist recommendation about the budget, and is in flat contradiction to the Keynesian idea that fiscal policy – i.e. the question of whether the budget should be balanced, or in surplus, or in deficit – needs to be tailored to the condition of the economy and its short- to medium-term prospects.

During the early years of the MTFS, fiscal policy was even more perverse than the basic monetarist prescription called for. This point can be simply demonstrated. Suppose that initially one has a state of full employment in the economy, and that the budget is in balance: expenditure equals revenue. Then suppose that, for whatever reason, the economy slides into recession. In a modern economy, certain 'automatic stabilizers' now come into operation. Those put on short-time working will suffer a loss of income, but their net incomes will fall less than their gross incomes because they will pay less income tax. Workers who lose their jobs altogether will not altogether cease to have an income, because they will draw unemployment benefit. In this way the tax and social security systems cushion the impact of recession. The other side of this coin, inevitably, is that when the economy goes into recession the government's budget will automatically go into deficit, as tax receipts fall and social security payments rise. If a government which believes that balancing the budget is at the very core of its economic policymaking reacts to this situation by trying to keep its budget balanced – by increasing taxes or cutting public expenditure – it will make things worse. Yet this was exactly the thrust of fiscal policy in the early 1980s.

The March 1981 budget was particularly notorious in this respect. The GDP had fallen by 2 per cent between 1979 and 1980 and was to fall by a further 1 per cent in 1981. Unemployment had risen by three-quarters of a million in 1980 and was to rise by another three-quarters of a million in 1981. Yet the 1981 budget significantly *tightened* fiscal policy, mainly by not raising tax allowances and thresholds in line with inflation – thus effectively increasing income tax – and partly by cutting government capital expenditure. By seeking to reduce effective demand at a time when the economy was in deep, and perhaps worsening, recession the government was pursuing a perverse, pro-cyclical fiscal policy of a kind that most economists had supposed had been abandoned for ever forty years earlier. Not content with this, Mrs Thatcher (who had personally been the architect of the March budget) tried in July to get the Cabinet to accept further large cuts in public expenditure, in addition to those already made over the past two years. This was, mercifully, one of the rare occasions on which she failed to carry the Cabinet with her.

Fortunately, the deflationary effects of the 1981 budget soon began to be outweighed, ironically enough, by a massive relaxation of monetary policy – something quite inconsistent with the logic of the MTFS. Late in 1980 Mrs Thatcher had been told by Professor Niehans, a distinguished Swiss monetarist she had consulted, that despite the huge overshooting of the sterling M3 targets, monetary policy in Britain was far too tight. Setting aside her legendary distrust of non-American foreigners (non-American foreign monetarists were evidently OK), she saw to it that interest rates were reduced from 16 per cent to 14 per cent in November 1980, and to 12 per cent in the March 1981 budget. This helped to stop output falling, and then to start it rising again; and this expansionary effect was later augmented by the fall in the pound that followed these sharp reductions in interest rates. Sterling's effective exchange rate fell by over 10 per cent during 1981, and although it was fairly stable during 1982, it fell again early in 1983. This increase in competitiveness must have had some effect in raising exports and restraining imports, though manufacturing industry had been so badly damaged by the government's policies that the growth of manufactured exports over the next few years was very slow, while the growth of manufactured imports was exceedingly rapid. A more important stimulus to economic activity than this improvement in competitiveness was undoubtedly the government's abolition of hire-purchase and other credit controls in the summer of 1982. In the short run this led to a big rise in expenditure on consumer durables, though in the longer run it was a major cause of the traumas of the late 1980s and early 1990s.

Thus the slow recovery that got under way in 1981 (and it was very slow – unemployment went on rising until the middle of 1986) occurred because the deflationary 1981 budget was out-gunned by other, more powerful, expansionary forces. This was something Mr Lawson, even a decade later, was unable to admit, continuing to decry a letter to *The Times* in which, late in March 1981, 364 economists had argued that the perverse fiscal policy the government was pursuing would deepen the recession. It was very soon after the 1981 budget that the recovery began, Mr Lawson has often asserted. Yes, but it took place despite, not because of, that budget.

By the middle of the 1980s the absurdities of the MTFS had become obvious even to its inventor, and a great deal less was heard of it. Nevertheless, securing and maintaining a very low rate of inflation continued to be the basic plank of the government's platform. If this could not be achieved by orthodox monetarist policies, because the Bank of England could not in practice control the money supply, or because different measures of the money supply behaved in quite different ways, or simply because the links between the money supply and the inflation rate were of high variability and ambiguous causality, then what was to be done?

In 1985 Mr Lawson hit on another idea: link sterling to the currency of a country with a traditionally low rate of inflation – i.e. to the Deutschemark. If this were done, then British managers and workers would have to ensure that price and wage increases were no greater than in Germany – or lose their businesses and their jobs to German competition. They could no longer be bailed out, as they had been on various occasions in the past, by a depreciation of sterling that saved them from the consequences of their inflationary behaviour.

In November 1985, therefore, Mr Lawson and a phalanx of heavyweights including the Deputy Prime Minister (William

Whitelaw), the Foreign Secretary and former Chancellor of the Exchequer (Sir Geoffrey Howe) and the Governor of the Bank of England, confronted Mrs Thatcher and unanimously demanded that Britain join the Exchange Rate Mechanism of the European Monetary System. Mrs Thatcher floored them with a single punch. She flatly refused, and swept imperiously from the room, leaving the eminent gentlemen as crestfallen as a bunch of schoolboys after a good ticking off from matron.

Mrs Thatcher's refusal to join the ERM in 1985 was fully consistent with her fundamental views about the economy. She believed in market forces and the operation of the price mechanism, and this was as true of the price of a currency as of anything else. The price of sterling should be determined by supply and demand, just like the price of cheese. Sterling should not be pegged to the Deutschemark or any other currency or group of currencies. It should continue to float freely, as it had done, more or less, since 1972. Such was her dominance of the Cabinet that she continued to impose this view for another five years, even though she seems to have been the only person of any weight in the government to hold it.

Thwarted in his desire to put the pound into the ERM, Mr Lawson eventually started to do the next best thing: to behave as though he had put it into the ERM. Phase Two of the macroeconomic policy pursued since 1979 (*Exchange Rate Rules OK?*) might be dated, in its weak form, from March 1987 (its strong form, when sterling actually joined the ERM, began only in October 1990). In March 1987 Mr Lawson embarked on a policy of 'shadowing' the Deutschemark – in other words, instructing the Bank of England to intervene in the foreign-exchange markets, buying or selling sterling as necessary in order to prevent it from moving very far below or above DM 3.00 to the pound.

He pursued this policy successfully for a year, until Mrs Thatcher put a stop to it. She had been slow to grasp some of the implications of the policy of shadowing the Deutschemark (indeed she subsequently, and implausibly, implied that she had not even been told about it). For various reasons, including a continuing decline in the value of the dollar, there was strong upward pressure on sterling from late 1987 onwards, and in order to keep this from raising the exchange rate the Bank of England had to intervene to sell large amounts of sterling in the markets. This led to a rise in the foreign-exchange reserves, and this in turn, in Mrs Thatcher's view, led to an increase in the money supply and was therefore inflationary. (In fact, a rise in the foreign-exchange reserves leads to a rise in the monetary base, and therefore in the money supply, only if it is not 'sterilized' by open-market operations; Lawson has claimed that the rise in the reserves in 1987–8 was fully sterilized in this way.)

Forbidden to keep the pound down by intervention, Mr Lawson tried to make it less attractive by cutting interest rates, bringing them down in three stages from 9 per cent in the middle of March 1988 to $7\frac{1}{2}$ per cent in the middle of May. This movement was soon put smartly into reverse, but the damage had been done: the interest-rate reductions earlier in the year had sent the markets the signal that continued expansion was wanted, at a time when the growth of credit was already getting wildly out of hand.

Mrs Thatcher and the monetarists who surrounded her often claimed that the cause of the inflationary explosion at the end of the 1980s was Mr Lawson's interference with market forces in trying to 'buck the market' by preventing sterling from rising, when that was what the markets wanted. In truth, the great credit boom was much more the consequence of Mrs Thatcher's dogmatic insistence that the market is always right. The deregulation of the financial system in the 1980s (in addition to paving the way for some colossal financial scandals in the early 1990s) had encouraged irresponsible behaviour by both borrowers and lenders.

The housing market provided a particularly vivid example of this. In the early 1980s banks were permitted to start lending for house purchase, and the traditional source of home loans, the building societies, were permitted to make loans for purposes that had nothing whatever to do with house purchase, such as buying a car or taking a holiday. (One building society, the Abbey National, actually turned itself into a bank.) Intense competition between these lenders developed on all fronts, but particularly for the lucrative and apparently risk free business of lending people money to buy their own houses. ('As safe as houses', the nation's subconscious was saying to it.) People with nothing much in the way of job security, and even less in the way of financial assets, found it quite easy to borrow a large proportion, sometimes all, of the money they needed to buy a house. And, as house prices started to rise rapidly – they doubled between 1985 and 1990 – home owners, not unreasonably, congratulated themselves on their sagacity, and felt wealthy enough to borrow, on credit cards or in other ways, in order to finance the purchase of more of the good things of life.

A few figures tell the story. Between the beginning of 1987 and the beginning of 1990 mortgage debt rose by 70 per cent. Over the same three-year period consumer credit and sterling M3 (the measure of the money supply to which the government had attached such importance at the beginning of the decade) both rose nearly as fast – by about 60 per cent. Market forces, largely unregulated, had promoted an expansion of credit far greater than made any kind of sense.

Mrs Thatcher's government rarely did things by halves. In the early 1980s both the monetary and the fiscal side of the MTFS had had a disastrous effect on the economy, plunging it into deep recession. Now fiscal policy, as well as monetary policy, had a disastrous effect in the other direction, helping to unleash a huge spending spree.

In 1986–7 the budget deficit, or PSBR, had finally come out at the 1 per cent of GDP (£4 billion) that Mr Lawson had first prescribed all those years ago. And it was going to stay there, he said in his 1987 budget speech. This permitted a cut in taxation of about £2.5 billion – i.e. a modest stimulus to the economy. From a Keynesian demand-management point of view, this was not an unreasonable judgement to make about fiscal policy at the time, though an objective assessment might suggest that an increase in public expenditure had a much higher priority than the 2p cut in income tax that the Chancellor introduced. But, mainly because of the credit boom, the economy expanded much more rapidly in 1987 than Lawson had anticipated. Tax revenue rose substantially, and the cost of paying unemployment benefits fell.

The consequence of this was that the actual budget outturn for 1987–8 was not the projected deficit of £4 billion, but a surplus (or Public Sector *Debt Repayment*) of £3 billion. And the projection for the next year (1988–9) was for a budget surplus, or PSDR, of £7 billion. In the interests of the basic objective of keeping the budget more or less in balance, Lawson reduced taxes by £4 billion in the 1988 budget, so that the budget surplus in 1988–9 would be only £3 billion, as in the previous year. (These tax cuts were extremely well received by the better off, who benefited not only from the increase in personal allowances at twice the rate of inflation and the reduction in the basic rate from 27 to 25 per cent but also – and very handsomely – from the reduction in the top tax rate from 60 per cent to 40 per cent. Forty per cent of the tax reductions went to the richest 5 per cent of the population.) It was in this 1988 budget speech that the fiscal objective was finally proclaimed to be an *exactly* balanced budget. After 1988–9, Lawson said, 'A zero PSBR will be the norm.'

The £4 billion fiscal stimulus administered in 1988 in the interests of balancing the budget, coming on top of the frenetic credit expansion that was already under way, led – in the same way as Mr Barber's measures in the early 1970s – to a much bigger rise in effective demand than the productive capacity of the economy, weakened by the factory closures and loss of skills caused by the recession of the early 1980s, was able to cope with. Imports flooded in. The balance of payments on current account, which (thanks to North Sea oil) had been in balance in 1986, ran a deficit of £4.5 billion in 1987, £16 billion in 1988 and £22 billion (about 5 per cent of the GDP) in 1989. Another consequence of the consumer boom was a rise in the inflation rate, from a little over 4 per cent in 1987 to about 5 per cent in 1988, 8 per cent in 1989, and over 10 per cent in the second half of 1990.

The rapid increase in money incomes led to higher tax revenues than had been expected. Consequently the outturn for 1988–9 was not the anticipated budget surplus of £3 billion but a budget surplus of £14 billion, or 3 per cent of the GDP. Even now Mr Lawson had not learned his lesson. Although he did at least resist the temptation, in his 1989 budget, to commit the ultimate folly of cutting taxes enough to bring the budget back into balance in 1989–90, he did nevertheless cut taxes by about £2 billion, thus stoking the inflationary fires even further. As in 1981, though in reverse, fiscal policy, dictated by the basic philosophy of monetarism and in pursuit of a balanced budget, was exactly the opposite of what was required.

The rise in the inflation rate in the second half of the 1980s was a consequence of the excessive increase in effective demand, reflected in the large fall in unemployment, from over 11 per cent in 1986 to under 6 per cent in 1990. The effect on inflation of this fall in unemployment was, predictably, the mirror image of the effect on inflation of the rise in unemployment in the first half of the decade. Workers, no longer fearful for their jobs, put in big wage demands; employers, foreseeing that large increases in profits were threatened not by a lack of demand but by a lack of skilled labour, were happy to concede them.

This rise in inflation, back into double figures in 1990, made a complete nonsense of the main objective the government had been pursuing for over a decade. Had not Mrs Thatcher put low inflation at centre-stage? Had not Mr Lawson said it would be 'judge and jury' of the monetary policy that lay at the heart of his stewardship of the economy? Had not devastating effects on employment, output and investment been tolerated in the interests of achieving a low and stable inflation rate?

The policies of the last decade had led up a blind alley. They had ended in fiasco. Nevertheless, something had to be done about inflation. But what? Higher taxes and a larger budget surplus were ruled out by the monetarist philosophy and by the underlying assumption that, contrary to common sense and everyday observation, the economy was self-stabilizing. So was any kind of direct control of credit (which, although difficult to operate in a world of free capital flows, was by no means impossible, as the experience of other European countries demonstrated). Incomes policies were, of course, unmentionable – had not an incomes policy, via the famous winter of discontent in

1978–9, brought down the last Labour government? In any case, after a decade of Thatcherism the unions, weakened though they had been by restrictive legislation, were in no mood for an incomes policy. 'In a free-for-all,' as a former trade union leader had warned a former Conservative government, 'we are part of the all.' The only answer was to raise interest rates, and this was what was done (prompting the comment from the former Conservative Prime Minister, Edward Heath, that Mr Lawson had put himself into the position of a one-club golfer).

Interest rates were raised from $7\frac{1}{2}$ per cent, where they had been (albeit briefly) in May 1988, to 13 per cent in November of that year and eventually to 15 per cent in October 1989. There they stayed for just over a year. This had traumatic effects on both business and household borrowers. Families that had borrowed heavily in the later 1980s, particularly for house purchase, were especially hard-hit, as mortgage interest rates, which had been below 10 per cent in the spring of 1988, rose to more than 15 per cent two years later. By 1990 many homebuyers were finding that their monthly repayments were much greater than they had budgeted for and 1990 was the year when unemployment started to rise again. Tens of thousands of breadwinners fell behind with their repayments, then lost their jobs, then defaulted on their mortgages, then saw their homes repossessed. Before long repossessions were running at a rate of 70,000 a year. Homelessness rose. House prices fell. Falling house prices soon led to over a million people – some estimates were closer to two million – finding that the value of their house was less than the amount of their mortgage, so they could not solve their problem by selling and moving to cheaper accommodation.

None of these traumas, however, had much immediate impact on inflation. The only answer to inflation, a large majority of the heavyweights in the Cabinet became increasingly convinced, was to do what they had wanted to do in November 1985: put sterling into the ERM of the European Monetary System. Eventually, under pressure from Mr Lawson's successor as Chancellor, Mr John Major, Mrs Thatcher reluctantly agreed. On 5 October 1990 (nicely timed to permit a reduction in interest rates to be proclaimed to the Conservative Party Conference), Major announced Britain's entry into the ERM. Phase Two (*Exchange Rate Rules OK?*) had moved into its strong, but final, stage.

Putting the pound into the ERM was a basically sensible move. For a widely held but second-rank currency like sterling the disadvantages of floating almost certainly outweighed the advantages. But any rejoicing at the move was instantly dissipated, at least in the minds of economists with any sense of history, by Mr Major's announcement that sterling's central rate against the Deutschemark was going to be DM 2.95. (This blow was only slightly cushioned by the fact that initially the permissible band each side of the central rate was going to be 6 per cent instead of the 2¼ per cent that applied to most other ERM currencies.)

This central rate of DM 2.95, apparently chosen unilaterally by Mr Major without any consultation with other European governments or central banks, was simply too high. If the DM 3.00 rate at which Mr Lawson had started to shadow the Deutschemark in March 1987 was about right (as, in so far as exactitude is possible in these matters, it probably was), DM 2.95 could not possibly be right in October 1990. Over the intervening three and a half years prices had risen by nearly 30 per cent in Britain but by only 8 per cent in Germany. If the same *real* exchange rate (or degree of competitiveness) was to be adopted in 1990 as Mr Lawson had favoured in 1987, the nominal exchange rate chosen should have been around DM 2.50. Britain had repeated exactly the same mistake as in 1925, when it went back on to the gold standard at the pre-war parity, ignoring the fact that in the meantime prices had risen far more in Britain than in the US, so that at the parity chosen Britain could not possibly compete. That move, scathingly criticized by Keynes at the time, had condemned Britain to another four or five years of heavy unemployment even before the onset of the slump in 1929. Much the same was to happen after October 1990. As unemployment rose from 1.8 million at the end of 1990 to 2.5 million at the end of 1991 and 2.8 million by the autumn of 1992, the gratuitous damage done by the unilateral decision to enter the ERM at an over-valued exchange rate became increasingly intolerable.

The British economy had turned down decisively in the middle of 1990, before the decision to join the ERM, and well before the beginning of the world recession. (The claim frequently made by the Chancellor and other ministers during the 1992 election campaign, that Britain's recession had been caused by the world recession, was either alarmingly ignorant or a severe case of being economical with the truth.) No attempt was made to use fiscal policy to fight falling output and rising unemployment. The 1991 budget, like the 1990 budget before it, was strictly neutral in its fiscal stance. The government's own finances had, of course, deteriorated as the slide into recession hit tax revenues and raised unemployment benefits, but the move that took place from budget surplus to budget deficit was entirely accounted for by this automatic element: no fiscal stimulus was administered to the economy at all. The most favourable comment that could be made was that if the government was failing to adopt the counter-cyclical fiscal policy the situation was crying out for, at least it was not engaging in the perverse pro-cyclical policy it had adopted in 1981.

A very small fiscal stimulus was administered in the 1992 budget, but since it came only a month before a general election, it was hardly surprising, and was more cosmetic than real. The broad thrust of fiscal policy continued to be neutral. But although the 1992 budget applied hardly any stimulus, the outlook for the economy was deteriorating so badly that the projected deficit (or PSBR) for 1992–3 was put at £28 billion, or $4\frac{1}{2}$ per cent of the GDP. The City of London was, predictably, 'shocked', and the price of gilt-edged securities plummeted. (The problem of conducting a rational fiscal policy in the face of the City's incorrigibly short time-horizons, lack of any sense of political and social priorities, and self-fulfilling prophecies of disaster whenever governments try to do anything it disapproves of, is discussed on pages 82–5.) There was, ostensibly, some relaxation of monetary policy from the autumn of 1990 onwards. Bank base rates, which had been at 15 per cent since October 1989, were reduced to 14 per cent in October 1990 and then, by a series of steps, to 10.5 per cent in the summer of 1991 and 10 per cent in the summer of 1992. But there was no fall in *real* interest rates (nominal interest rates minus inflation) between mid-1990 and mid-1992 because meanwhile the inflation rate fell from around 10 per cent to around 4 per cent. And real *long-term* interest rates – those most likely to be relevant to investment decisions – actually rose significantly over this two-year period.

In short, little was done to prevent Britain from sliding into deeper recession. The underlying monetarist philosophy still prevailed. Fiscal policy should be neutral, in the sense that there should be no changes in tax rates or government expenditure in an attempt to influence the level of economic activity (though it was now grudgingly accepted that temporary budget deficits might have to be tolerated during a recession). And the rise in the money supply should be kept slow and steady. (M0, the government's new favourite measure of the money supply, which simply consisted of notes and coins, proved very well behaved by this criterion: it grew at a fairly steady rate of 2–3 per cent a year throughout 1990 and 1991.) Meanwhile, consumers' expenditure, accounting for two-thirds of the GDP, fell by 2 per cent in 1991 and declined further in 1992. Investment, which had already dropped in 1990, fell by 10 per cent in 1991 and continued to fall in 1992. The volume of exports, restrained by the overvaluation of the pound and later by the slow-down in the world economy, showed little growth after the middle of 1990.

For more than two years after the beginning of the recession in mid-1990 the government did not merely fail to engage in the kind of demand management policies employed by all post-war governments until 1979; it actually dug itself deeper into its bunker. By early 1992 the Prime Minister (Mr Major) had started to talk of 'zero inflation' as the government's basic economic objective. Quite apart from the fact that Britain had not had zero inflation for more than fifty years (nor had most other countries), to make its achievement not just an aim but the basic aim of government policy at a time when the slide into recession was gathering pace suggested an alarming lack of contact with the real world. This impression was compounded when the *Sunday Times* revealed on 2 August that Mr Major had been talking of the day – not far off, he implied – when sterling would replace the Deutschemark as the benchmark currency at the heart of the European Monetary System.

The strains within the ERM had been growing greater. One reason was implicit in any fixed exchange-rate mechanism: inflation rates tend to be higher in some countries than in others, so that an unchanged *nominal* exchange rate (like DM 2.95 to the pound) necessarily implies changes in *real* exchange rates, which are what affect competitiveness.

But another factor was also at work. The dramatic reunification of Germany in October 1990 had created inflationary pressures there, essentially because the former East Germans, subsidized by their Western brothers, were now consuming more than they were producing. The German government's failure to deal with these pressures by tightening fiscal policy threw on to the Bundesbank most of the burden of keeping down inflation (in its view, anyway). In an over-zealous attempt (see page 50) to control the growth of the money supply, the Bundesbank kept on raising short-term interest rates until they reached the historically high level of almost 10 per cent. This put an effective floor under interest rates throughout the rest of Europe. No one expected that the Deutschemark would ever be devalued in terms of any other ERM currency, so if they could get 10 per cent by holding Deutschemarks, why should anyone hold any other European currency that yielded less than 10 per cent?

It was no good the Chancellor of the Exchequer (Mr Norman Lamont) saying, as he did on 10 July 1992, 'The ERM is not an optional extra, an add-on to be jettisoned at the first hint of trouble. It is, and will remain, at the very centre of our macro-economic strategy.' The fact was that the financial markets were increasingly taking the view that currencies such as the pound and the Italian lira would have to be devalued within the ERM, or leave the system altogether. This was partly because they continued to look distinctly overvalued, and partly because the political strain, at a time of ever-rising unemployment, of keeping interest rates at the level needed to support their existing ERM parities would eventually reach breaking point. And so indeed it proved. Over the weekend of 12–13 September European Finance Ministers agreed a 7 per cent devaluation of the lira within the ERM. Mr Lamont refused to hear of any realignment of sterling. (But he was only echoing his Prime Minister, who, in a speech to the Scottish Confederation of British Industry a few days earlier, had categorically – and gratuitously – ruled out the idea, talking of such a realignment as 'the soft option, the devaluer's option, the inflationary option ... a betrayal of our future'. The result was Black Wednesday (16 September), when Mr Lamont jacked up interest rates first (at 11.00 a.m.) to 12 per cent and later (at 2.15 p.m.) to 15 per cent, while the Bank of England intervened in the markets and bought £15–£20 billion of sterling – perhaps even more – in a futile attempt to maintain the doomed parity. (The Bank of England's kamikaze-style intervention cost Britain at least £2–£3 billion. This is the difference between the price at which the Bank of England sold dollars, Deutschemarks and other foreign currencies in order to defend the pound, and the price at which it had to buy them back later in order to replenish the reserves.) By the evening of Black Wednesday the game was up. The pound was removed altogether from the ERM – in other words, floated.

The opportunity to realign sterling within the ERM, at a realistic rate which the combined resources of all the European central banks would be committed to defending, had thus been lost. (Indeed Britain's actions might turn out to have done much damage to the ERM itself – even, perhaps, to have set in motion forces that would eventually destroy it.) Instead, the value of the pound would once again be mainly determined by market forces, and in circumstances much less favourable than those of the early 1980s, when large sales of North Sea oil provided Britain with the foreign-exchange ammunition required to defend the value of the pound, should that prove necessary.

Thus began Phase Three of the post-1979 economic strategy. What ruled initially was, if not quite chaos, at any rate confusion and indecision, not to mention a touch of farce. Neither the money supply (as in Phase One) nor the exchange rate (as in Phase Two) was going to be targeted. Nothing more was heard of sterling as the benchmark currency of Europe. The fixed parity against the Deutschemark, for two years at the very centre of the government's economic strategy, was forgotten in an instant, and replaced by a fulsome welcome for the fall in the exchange rate, which now gave an opportunity to British exports. Zero inflation was suddenly whisked out of sight and replaced by a range of 1–4 per cent inflation (the Chancellor saying sternly that he had in mind something towards the low end of this range). Prime Minister and Chancellor (both still holding on to their jobs, regardless of everything) popped up all over the place, talking of a strategy for recovery, for growth, for jobs. But what this strategy was going to consist of remained unclear. Interest rates were reduced, first to 9 per cent, then to 8 per cent, then to 7 per cent, then to 6 per cent. But relying on lower interest rates alone to get the economy out of a recession was, as Keynes had once remarked, like pushing on a piece of string. And these lower interest rates were not without serious risks: the only logical reason for anyone to put money into sterling at 6 per cent if they could get nearly 10 per cent on Deutschemarks would be the expectation of an appreciation of sterling against the Deutschemark. For this expectation to be created, sterling would have to overshoot downwards, below what was regarded in the markets as the equilibrium parity. Such a downward float could easily get out of hand, creating the danger of an inflationary spiral that might prove very difficult and painful to bring under control.

Some coherence was eventually given to the third, post-Black Wednesday, phase of economic policy in the Chancellor's Autumn Statement of 12 November 1992, which marked at least a partial return to economic sanity. In particular, it became clear that the simplistic notion that inflation was caused by increases in the money supply had been jettisoned. Although the Phase Two recipe for dealing with inflation (pegging sterling to the Deutschemark) had been abandoned, there was to be no return to the Phase One recipe of monetary targeting. Instead, the behaviour of the money supply was merely to be *monitored* – i.e. treated as one of the many indicators to be watched by the government for evidence of the way the economy was moving.

This was perfectly sensible. (By this time the government, in its restless search for the perfect measure of the money supply, had switched its affections from Mo to M4; it seemed only a matter of time before it would be courting M6 or M25.)

Just how inflation was going to be kept under control was left unclear, despite the obvious fact that the effective devaluation of sterling of well over 10 per cent would have an inflationary effect through higher import prices. Interest rates would be used as necessary, said the Chancellor, ignoring the fact that any upward movement of interest rates would only deepen the recession. He announced a $1\frac{1}{2}$ per cent limit on pay increases in the public sector, but this was done in order to hold down public expenditure, not as part of a comprehensive incomes policy. Apart from some exhortation, no actual measures to restrain the growth of pay in the private sector were proposed, despite the imperative need to prevent the beneficial effect on the balance of payments of sterling's devaluation being rapidly eroded by higher inflation. The recession did, of course, put a damper on wage and salary increases in the private sector, but whether these would be low enough to prevent a rise in the inflation rate seemed doubtful.

Also finally abandoned, in the November 1992 Autumn Statement, was the idea that had dictated the fiscal side of the Medium Term Financial Strategy: that the growth of the money supply was determined by the size of the PSBR, and that the aim of fiscal policy should therefore be to have a PSBR that was zero or close to it. The Chancellor confirmed his acceptance that the budgetary position was bound to vary over the cycle and that it was only over the cycle as a whole, or in the medium term, that it was sensible to require the budget to be balanced. In recession there were bound to be budget deficits, and to attempt to reduce them (as in 1981) would only make the recession worse. Thus he accepted, with reasonable equanimity, that the PSBR might be £37 billion, or 6.25 per cent of the GDP, in 1992–3 and £44 billion, or 7 per cent of the GDP, in 1993–4. (This latter figure was subsequently raised, to the accompaniment of much pious lip-pursing and head-shaking, to £50 billion.)

Unfortunately, he refused to pursue the logic of this view to its conclusion. These budget deficits were mainly the consequence of the fall in tax revenue and the rise in social security benefits caused by the recession; they reflected to only a minimal extent the discretionary measures, in the form of tax cuts or public expenditure increases, needed to deal with the recession. Although a few useful measures were adopted, the sum total of fiscal stimulus announced in the November 1992 statement was £4 billion over three years – less than $\frac{1}{4}$ per cent of GDP per year. 'I do not believe,' said Mr Lamont solemnly, 'that governments can spend their way out of recession.' A return of 'confidence' is the only thing that will lead to more jobs, he kept on saying. On the contrary, the only thing that seemed likely to lead to an early return of confidence was the creation of more jobs – and this had to be done by government action to get the economy moving again.

The 1992 Autumn Statement was based on the same fundamental error that had characterized the Conservative government's economic policy ever since 1979: the belief that market forces can invariably be relied on to bring the economy back to full employment. Keynes might never have lived.

A critique of the monetarist philosophy, with its insistence that the economy should be left to the operation of market forces, would no doubt carry less weight if the economic record since 1979 had been a successful one. But this was not the case. In most respects it was abysmal.

Unemployment, the fundamental touchstone of a satisfactory economic policy from 1945 until the mid-1970s, averaged 9 per cent between 1979 and 1992. On the old definition of unemployment, however, it would have averaged about 11 per cent – compared with a figure of less than 2 per cent between 1945 and 1970, and 4 per cent in the 1970s. In absolute numbers, unemployment was 1.3 million in May 1979 and 3 million at the beginning of 1993. The economic waste of having more than a tenth of the labour force out of work is self-evident. Less obvious, but even less forgivable, is the damage done to the cohesiveness of society, and the ruin of millions of individual lives.

A low, even zero, inflation rate often seemed to be the be-all and end-all of economic policy between 1979 and 1992. Yet over this period inflation averaged 7 per cent. This was significantly lower than the average figure for the 1970s – 13 per cent – but substantially higher than the 4 per cent rate between 1945 and 1970. It was also higher than in other comparable countries. Between 1979 and 1992 the inflation rate was 6 per cent in France, 5 per cent in the US, 3 per cent in Germany and 2½ per cent in Japan.

A dynamic, strongly growing economy was supposed to be the main reward of a policy of deregulating, privatizing and generally trusting in the benevolence of market forces, but the growth record – despite the uncovenanted manna from heaven represented by North Sea oil – was dismal. In 1992 the GDP was only 22 per cent higher than it had been in 1979, an average growth rate of 1.5 per cent a year. This may be criticized as a peak-to-trough comparison and therefore unfair, though it seems legitimate to ask who caused the trough? But even the peak-to-peak comparison (1979–1990) yields a rise of only 25 per cent – an average annual growth rate of 2.1 per cent. This compares with a growth rate of 2 per cent a year in the despised 1970s (and 2.8 per cent in the 1960s). No miracles here.

The discovery of huge amounts of oil under the North Sea had been expected by many observers to put an end to the chronic balance-of-payments difficulties that have plagued Britain since the end of the war. Not a bit of it. Over the six years 1980–85 there was a cumulative current-account surplus of £23 billion. But the strengthening of Britain's external financial position that this represented was obliterated over the subsequent six years, 1987–92, when there was a cumulative current-account deficit of £78 billion. It was as if a hard-pressed family man had unexpectedly inherited a fortune and then squandered it in a few days at the gaming tables of Las Vegas.

High unemployment, an inflation rate that was above those of Britain's industrial rivals, a rate of growth that was lower than even Britain had achieved over the previous four decades, a cumulative balance-of-payments deficit which, according to government statistics published in September 1992, had helped to reduce Britain's net overseas wealth from £100 billion in 1986 to zero by 1990 – as if all this were not enough, the distribution of income worsened dramatically in the decade after 1979. This was partly because the gross incomes of those at the top of the income scale rose more than the average, and partly because of the regressive nature of the government's changes in taxation and social security benefits. In real terms the post-tax income of the top fifth rose by 40 per cent between 1979 and 1989; the real income of the poorest fifth actually *fell* by 5 per cent. The numbers living in poverty (defined as those with a disposable income of less than half the average) were 5 million in 1979 and 12 million in 1989. The latest statistics (June 1993) indicate that the gap between rich and poor widened even further between 1989 and 1991.

According to the historian Tacitus, the Celtic chief Calgacus, surveying the activities of the Romans in Scotland in AD 83, observed, 'They make a wilderness and call it peace' (*solitudinem faciunt, pacem appellant*). Given the chance to survey the activities of the monetarist-inspired British government some 1,900 years later, as dole queues lengthened and increasing swathes of the country became derelict wastelands of abandoned factories, unoccupied offices, boarded-up shops and repossessed houses, Calgacus might have been moved to repeat himself.

5

THE ROLE OF THE BUDGET

'For 1980–81, the year which is drawing to a close, the PSBR is now forecast to emerge at £13.5 billion, or 6 per cent of the GDP . . . This year's budget-making exercise has started from the basis of a forecast for the PSBR in 1981–2 of no less than £14 billion. I am in no doubt that to begin the year with the intention of borrowing as much as £14 billion would be irresponsible . . . I have concluded that it would be right to provide for a PSBR in 1981–2 of some £10.5 billion, which is a little more than 4 per cent of the GDP.'
—Budget Speech by Sir Geoffrey Howe, Chancellor of the Exchequer, 10 March 1981.

'I expect the PSBR in the current year to rise to around £37 billion. Of course, that is high, but borrowing is bound to rise in a recession; and it would be damaging to seek to prevent it from doing so.'
—Autumn Statement by Mr Norman Lamont, Chancellor of the Exchequer, 12 November 1992.

So the government had learned something between 1981 and 1992.

'I do not believe that governments can spend their way out of recession.'
—Autumn Statement by Mr Norman Lamont, Chancellor of the Exchequer, 12 November 1992.

But not very much.

This chapter argues that it is rational for a government to use fiscal policy in a discretionary way, taking deliberate action to run budget deficits or budget surpluses, depending on the short- to medium-term outlook for the economy. If the economy appears to be sliding into recession, the government should stand ready to intervene by reducing taxation or increasing public expenditure. This intervention should be *over and above* the effects on tax revenues and social security expenditures that are purely *cyclical* – i.e. the *automatic* consequences of a move into recession. The budget should not merely be allowed to move into deficit during a recession. It should be deliberately *made* to move into deficit – a bigger deficit than would occur automatically – in order to prevent, or at least cure, a recession.

The same applies, of course, in reverse. If the sum of individual and business spending decisions looks likely to exceed the economy's capacity to produce (as it did from early 1988 onwards), leading to a rise in the inflation rate or a balance-of-payments crisis, the government should step in to increase taxes or cut public expenditure. This will result in a bigger budget surplus (or smaller deficit) than would be the automatic result of the rising tax revenue and falling social security payments associated with a boom, but that is what the situation requires.

Fiscal policy is essentially a matter of the relationship between government expenditure and government revenue – the question of whether the budget should be balanced, or in deficit, or in surplus. This does not, however, mean that the *composition* of expenditure and revenue is unimportant. The nature of the tax structure (how far, for example, it relies on direct rather than indirect taxes) and the form of public expenditure (how far, for example, it consists of social security benefits and of the provision of free or subsidized services) will both have effects on the distribution of income; and this – quite apart from its intrinsic importance – will affect the level of demand in the economy.

Suppose that total government expenditure equals total government revenue. The budget is balanced. Disciples of monetarism, such as Mr Lawson and Mr Lamont, sing in their baths. Suppose, further, that under the pressure of public opinion the government decides to increase child benefit in line with inflation (something the British government failed to do between 1987 and 1991) and finances this by effectively increasing capital gains tax (for example, by ceasing to index it to inflation, in the way that it has been indexed since 1982). The Lawsons and Lamonts are not entirely happy about this because they think that taxes should be as low as possible. Nevertheless, what matters most to them is that the budget remains in balance, and they still sing in their baths, though perhaps slightly out of tune. Effective demand, however, does not remain the same, because most of the increase in child benefit will be spent, as it always is, whereas most of the increased yield of capital gains tax will come out of savings: those affected will not significantly reduce their consumption. Thus, although the budget stays balanced, effective demand is increased.

This is one reason why the notion that a balanced budget is good and an unbalanced one bad is excessively simple-minded. Another has been important in recent years. Since 1979 most of Britain's nationalized industries have been sold off or 'privatized'. The proceeds of these sales, of the order of £5–£6 billion a year, have been counted as *negative* public expenditure. This bizarre public-accounting practice has probably been a good thing, because it has permitted a higher level of genuine public expenditure, on goods and services and on transfer payments, to be treated as consistent with a given target for the PSBR. Nevertheless, the privatization of an industry does not represent a real reduction in public expenditure any more than nationalization represents a real increase in public expenditure. Essentially all that happens when something like British Gas is privatized is a swapping of assets. Institutional and individual investors now hold some British Gas shares in their portfolios instead of other equities, or government securities, or cash. This no doubt has some minor effects on the prices and yields of certain classes of assets, but makes little difference to effective demand. Unlike a £5 billion sale of publicly-owned assets, a £5 billion cut in social security benefits, or in health or educational expenditure, would mean a significant fall in the level of demand.

Budget surpluses tend to be uncontroversial. Chancellors who achieve them pat themselves on the back and point out that they are repaying some of the National Debt (which indeed they are: whether this is an appropriate thing to be doing is a different matter). It is budget deficits which are contentious. Mrs Thatcher was fond of comparing the nation's accounts with those of a household; only an imprudent housewife, the message went, allows her outgoings to exceed her income. Budget deficits seem to be regarded in some quarters as close to the ultimate sin. 'How are you going to pay for it?' is the cry. This matter must now be discussed more fully.

Hostility to budget deficits which are deliberately engineered by the government is rooted, consciously or not, in the classical or monetarist assumptions about the working of the economy. If the normal condition of the economy is one of full employment, it is easy to see why a budget deficit is regarded as undesirable. By spending more than it is collecting in taxes, the government is absorbing more resources than it is paying for. Where are these resources to come from? Given that there is full employment, and thus no way of increasing overall output in the short run, there are only three possibilities. One is that resources will be diverted away from what are assumed to be more profitable uses in the private sector. The second is that the extra resources come from abroad – i.e. that the counterpart of government borrowing will be a balance-of-payments deficit on current account. The third possibility – if resources can be diverted neither from the private sector nor from abroad – is that prices will have to rise to absorb the difference between total expenditure and total output. In each case, or even in a combination of these cases, the outcome can reasonably be seen as undesirable.

Once it is accepted, however, that the economy is not self-stabilizing at full employment, the picture changes completely. A government which runs a budget deficit in order to prevent or cure a recession is not absorbing more than its share of a fixed quantity of resources. It is calling into use resources – men and machinery – that would otherwise be standing idle. That is how the excess of expenditure over revenue is 'paid for': from production that would not otherwise have taken place.

The discussion in the last few paragraphs has been in terms of real resources, which seems reasonable enough, since that is ultimately what economic policy is all about. But that does not necessarily dispose of the problem of actually *financing* budget deficits, in the sense of raising the necessary money on acceptable terms. Before addressing this issue, however, a more general argument about budget deficits needs to be examined.

This relates to what is often called a 'structural' deficit. This is a deficit that is neither a 'cyclical' deficit – the consequence of the automatic fall in tax receipts and rise in social security payments that occur in a recession – nor the kind of deficit that results from deliberate steps, of the kind just discussed, to prevent or cure a recession. A structural deficit is one that exists even when the economy is at full employment: a chronic deficit, which requires the government to borrow money every year, and which inevitably implies a steady increase in the size of the National Debt.

There is a widespread presumption that a structural deficit is a bad thing. Such a presumption is not unreasonable, and should be not lightly discarded. But it should not be accepted blindly either. This is, admittedly, dangerous territory. Structural deficits lurk around every corner in a democracy, because politicians love to cut taxes and increase expenditure; it is how they get re-elected. Africa and Latin America are full of countries where structural budget deficits have led to disaster of one sort or another. And, nearer home, Italy's chronic inability to collect enough tax to pay for its government expenditure has been a source of trouble, and jokes, for decades. But this does not alter the fact that to run a structural deficit – i.e. to finance expenditure by borrowing, even on quite a long-term basis – can be a perfectly rational thing for a government to do, just as it can be a perfectly rational thing for an individual, or a business, or a country, to do. It all depends on what the money is used for – or, more technically, on the real rate of return on the expenditure compared with what would have been the real rate of return on the borrowed funds if they had been used in some other way.

The point can most easily be seen in the case of a business. A firm which borrows from a bank or through the stock market at 10 per cent a year in order to finance an investment that yields 20 per cent a year is doing precisely what successful firms are supposed to do, and is likely to grow and prosper. Similarly (until the excesses of the late 1980s, anyway) a family that borrows to buy a house on a mortgage is usually behaving perfectly sensibly. It is borrowing to acquire an asset whose total yield – including, in this case, the psychological as well as the financial benefits of owning its own home – exceeds the interest payments on the loan. On a much larger scale, a country which runs a chronic balance-of-payments deficit on current account, financing this deficit by borrowing from abroad at relatively low rates of interest and investing this money in projects with high rates of return, is behaving in a completely rational way. This is exactly what the United States did in the nineteenth century. American enterprises borrowed large sums from Britain (where rates of interest were relatively low) and invested them in projects, such as the railways, where rates of return were very high. The result was a chronic American balance-of-payments deficit on current account and a corresponding British surplus. But in the circumstances this imbalance benefited both countries.

The same considerations apply to a government. If a government spends more than its total tax revenue at a time of full employment (i.e. runs a structural deficit), it may be behaving irresponsibly, but it may not: it depends on what it does with the money it borrows. Suppose the money were being spent on old-age pensions (in the sense that, if there were no structural deficit, old-age pensions would be lower by the amount of the structural deficit). This would clearly be irresponsible, particularly if the country had an ageing population. If old-age pensions are too low, an increase in them should be financed by an increase in taxes or national insurance contributions, not by borrowing. If, on the other hand, the money borrowed to finance the structural deficit is being devoted to projects with a higher real rate of return than the private-sector projects that are being displaced (because private-sector savings are now being lent to the government to finance its budget deficit, rather than being invested in the private sector), its behaviour is perfectly rational.

The most obvious area where this criterion is likely to be satisfied is that of large-scale infrastructure projects. The overall rate of return (including social benefits, such as a reduction in congestion and pollution, as well as the private benefits) on urban mass-transit systems, for example, particularly in the London area, could hardly fail to be higher than the overall rate of return on much private-sector investment. Thus a government which ran a structural budget deficit, borrowing in order to finance this kind of capital investment, would be behaving in a way that promoted one of its basic economic objectives – achieving a respectable rate of growth. (In practice it might not be just the private-sector projects with the lowest rate of return that were displaced; but that would be a reflection of resource misallocation *within* the private sector, calling for improved investment appraisal techniques there, and having no bearing on the case for a government budget deficit.)

This argument prompts calls, from time to time, for the government's accounts to be recast in a way that makes it clearer how much expenditure might be classified as capital or investment expenditure, as opposed to current expenditure. It would then be easier to see whether, and how far, structural budget deficits were of the benevolent kind just discussed. There is much to be said for this proposal. It would help to demonstrate to those inclined to think that all public expenditure is a form of (often wasteful) consumption that a lot of public expenditure is productive investment, just as when a company in the private sector builds a car factory or a supermarket.

Nevertheless, the proposal would need to be implemented with care, to avoid reinforcing the belief that government expenditure that is *not* capital expenditure is in some way undesirable and needs to be kept to a minimum. In practice, much government expenditure that would clearly be classified as *current* rather than *capital* may yield high rates of return even on purely economic criteria (and would, in fact, be classified as 'investment' by some economists). Subsidies to research and development expenditure are one obvious example. The pay of those engaged in educating and training the labour force (often described as 'investment in human capital') is another. There are both theoretical and empirical reasons to suppose that market forces underprovide research and development (R & D) expenditures, as well as both education and training. If a government were to run a structural deficit in order to provide the socially optimal amount of R & D and education and training, it would probably be promoting, not hampering, an increase in living standards.

Two further points need to be made before leaving the subject of structural deficits. First, the use of the term 'structural deficit' should be accompanied by a government (or perhaps non-government) health warning. For whether a budget deficit is structural or simply cyclical depends crucially on what one thinks is the full employment level of output. If a pessimistic view is taken of this, and it is assumed that unemployment cannot be brought down below, say, 8 per cent without causing inflation to accelerate, then any deficit that occurs at this unemployment rate will be called 'structural'. But if it were assumed, more optimistically, that the unemployment rate could safely be brought down to – and maintained at – 4 per cent, and if at this unemployment rate there were no deficit (because of higher tax revenue and lower social security payments), then clearly the deficit that was incurred when unemployment was 8 per cent would be cyclical, not structural. In short, whether a deficit is structural or not lies to a considerable extent in the eye of the beholder.

Secondly, notwithstanding all that has been said above, it is entirely possible that in 1993 Britain does have a structural deficit that cannot be justified by the kind of arguments just discussed. (According to the OECD *Economic Outlook*, December 1992, all the G7 countries except Japan were in this position in 1992.) Such a deficit needs to be reduced or eliminated because by definition it is pre-empting resources that would be better used elsewhere. (In Britain's case the resources are badly needed to eliminate the apparently chronic balance-of-payments deficit.) Public expenditure has been squeezed so much in Britain in recent years that most of the brunt of eliminating a structural budget deficit would probably have to be borne by higher taxes. The phasing out of mortgage-interest tax relief, the extension of the 9 per cent employees' National Insurance contribution (which is income tax in all but name) beyond its present £21,840 a year income ceiling, higher taxes on petrol – all these make sense in terms of economic efficiency, equity or environmental protection. But the time to start reducing a structural deficit is when the economy is recovering strongly from recession, and tax increases or reductions in public expenditure are needed to make room for higher exports or more private investment. To take steps to reduce a structural budget deficit during a recession is thoroughly perverse; it only intensifies and prolongs the agony.

One way in which a government can finance a deficit is by borrowing from the banking system – i.e. increasing the money supply. There is nothing intrinsically wrong with financing a deficit in this way, as many people assume: it depends on the circumstances. If the economy is in recession, all that the government is doing, in borrowing from the banking system and spending this money, is taking action to increase effective demand and bring the economy back up to full utilization of its capacity. There is no reason why this process should be inflationary in the traditional demand–pull, 'too much money chasing too few goods' sense, because the extra money in the system will be matched by increased output and therefore extra goods. What *is* true is that, as the economy moves out of recession and back up to full employment, the fall in unemployment may create a climate in which inflationary wage increases are more likely to be demanded and conceded, and prices are more likely to be increased in order to restore profit margins. That is, indeed, what happened between 1986 and 1990. But this has nothing to do with the fact that the government is running a budget deficit and financing it by increasing the money supply; it is a reflection of the long-standing and unfortunate tendency – more marked in Britain than in many other countries – for money wages to rise substantially faster than productivity, particularly when unemployment is low or falling. Unless the nation is willing to tolerate high, and perhaps rising, unemployment for ever, this is a problem that ultimately has to be dealt with by some form of incomes policy. It will not be solved by refusing to implement an expansionary fiscal policy, financed if necessary by borrowing from the banking system, at times of recession.

The other main way in which a government can finance a budget deficit is by selling securities to (i.e. borrowing from) the non-bank private sector, which consists of insurance companies, pension funds, investment trusts, individuals, etc. This is, in fact, the usual method of financing a deficit: it was pointed out on page 49 that virtually all of the budget deficits of the late 1970s were financed like this, and in 1985 Mr Lawson decreed (unnecessarily and perhaps unwisely, since it is a completely arbitrary rule) that henceforth all budget deficits should be fully 'funded' in this way.

It may appear that there is something more virtuous about a budget deficit, or PSBR, that is funded than a budget deficit that is financed by borrowing from the banking system. But those whose faces are firmly set against a discretionary fiscal policy which involves budget deficits have objections to such deficits even when they are fully funded. These objections can be broken down into two different arguments.

The first argument is that by borrowing from the non-bank private sector the government is increasing the National Debt, and thus imposing a burden on future generations, who will have to service this extra debt.

It is undoubtedly true that by funding the budget deficit, or PSBR, in this way, the government is adding to the National Debt. The non-bank private sector will now hold more government bonds than it did before, and the need to pay interest on this extra debt will mean that in future years the government will have to collect more in taxes than it otherwise would have. But the belief that this will necessarily constitute a 'burden' on future generations is mistaken. If all other things remained equal, more government borrowing, implying higher government interest payments in the future, would of course mean a greater burden on future taxpayers. But other things do not remain equal. The whole point of the government running a budget deficit is to maintain, or soon return to, a full employment level of output, instead of permitting the economy to slide into a possibly deep and long-lasting recession. By its actions the government is ensuring a higher level of output and incomes in the present – and therefore, through the effects of this on investment and growth, a higher level of output and incomes in the future. It is true that future generations will have to pay more taxes, but they will be doing so out of a higher income.

There is no reason why their taxes should rise as a proportion of their income, and, since their income will be higher, they will be better off. To put it another way, there is no reason to expect that a higher National Debt means a higher ratio of National Debt to GDP; and if there is no increase in this ratio, there is no increase in the burden on future generations.

The second objection to financing a budget deficit by sales of government bonds is that these bond sales will 'crowd out' an equivalent amount of private-sector investment. If the non-bank private sector is to absorb more bonds, the argument goes, it will be willing to do so only at a lower price; and this is just another way of saying that it will do so only at a higher rate of interest. This will raise long-term interest rates generally, and will mean that some private-sector investment projects that were profitable before will not be profitable now, and so will not be undertaken. At the end of the day the budget deficit will not have resulted in any net increase in output or employment in the economy; all it will have done is to replace some private-sector investment expenditure by an equivalent amount of (allegedly less productive) public expenditure.

This argument (which is the same as the infamous 'Treasury view' relentlessly attacked by Keynes in the 1920s) is easily disposed of. If the economy is at full employment, any extra public expenditure will, by definition, displace some private expenditure (unless it simply leads to a rise in imports). But no government in its senses will engage in an expansionary fiscal policy at a time of full employment. Undertaken at a time of recession, there is no reason why a higher level of public expenditure should displace private expenditure: there is room for more of both. The depressing effect on private investment of any increase in interest rates resulting from more sales of government securities is likely to be outweighed by the stimulative effects of the higher level of government expenditure and its multiplier effects on incomes and consumption. Private investment is more likely to rise in these circumstances than to fall. And in any case, if higher interest rates really were likely to lead to a lower level of private investment, this merely demonstrates that the government should not be financing its deficit by sales of gilt-edged securities; it should be financing it by increasing the money supply.

The arguments which have just been answered, objecting to a discretionary fiscal policy that leads to a deliberate budget deficit at times of recession, are all coherent and rational arguments; they just happen to be mistaken. Much more difficult to deal with are the irrational arguments – one might almost say the mindless Pavlovian responses – that dominate the behaviour of the financial markets. Nevertheless, these arguments can be answered too. (For the sake of brevity, the term 'a budget deficit' will be used as shorthand for 'a budget deficit that is bigger than it would otherwise be, because the government implements a deliberately expansionary fiscal policy', and the terms 'financial markets' and 'City' will be used interchangeably.)

The City's basic presumption is that a budget deficit is inflationary. Any City worthy or whizz-kid capable of articulating his or her reasons for believing this would probably argue, as did Mr Lawson when inventing the MTFS, that a budget deficit leads to an increase in the money supply and that an increase in the money supply leads to inflation. Both these propositions were discussed in earlier chapters, and both were dismissed; and even the Conservative government had abandoned these simplistic notions by 1992. (It is, of course, true, as was emphasized earlier, that a budget deficit is likely to be inflationary if introduced at a time when the economy is already at full employment, because effective demand will then exceed productive capacity; but that is not the case under discussion.)

As was noted above, a budget deficit financed by sales of government bonds will lead to some rise in long-term interest rates, because extra bonds will have to be sold at a lower price, and this implies a higher interest rate. But there is now effectively a single world capital market, and this is so large in relation to any discretionary British budget deficit of the kind under discussion that the rise in interest rates needed to accommodate the extra borrowing is likely to be negligible. There is, however, a further problem. Regardless of how far the deficit is financed by bond sales and how far by an increase in the money supply, the

City's belief that a budget deficit is inflationary (however misguided this belief may be) may itself put further upward pressure on interest rates in Britain. This is because a higher inflation rate would require an increase in *nominal* interest rates in order to achieve the same *real* interest rates. Thus the City's exaggerated fears about the impact of the budget deficit on inflation may lead to a rise in nominal, and therefore in real, interest rates that is greater than the actual circumstances justify.

The only complete solution to this problem – as Robert Lowe, Chancellor of the Exchequer from 1868–73, observed about the extension of the franchise in the 1867 Reform Bill – is to educate our masters. But a rational fiscal policy cannot wait until we have done that. In the meantime there are two things the government can do that would help with the problem.

First, it can finance some or all of the budget deficit not by sales of conventional gilt-edged securities, but by sales of index-linked securities. With a conventional gilt the redemption value of the certificate is a fixed nominal sum (normally £100). With an index-linked gilt, on the other hand, the redemption value is linked to the retail price index (as is the annual yield), which means that the inflation risk is borne by the government, not by the investor. If, for example, a budget deficit is financed by issuing a conventional gilt yielding 7 per cent at a time when the inflation rate is 4 per cent, the investor reckons on achieving a 3 per cent *real* rate of return. But if the very existence of the budget deficit causes the City, however irrationally, to believe that the inflation rate will rise to 5 per cent, the investor's prospective real rate of return will be reduced by a third. Hence he demands a nominal yield not of 7 per cent but of 8 per cent, and nominal interest rates will have to rise accordingly if the government is to succeed in funding its budget deficit. With an index-linked gilt, on the other hand, most of the rise in the inflation rate, if it occurs, will be reflected in an increase in the price at which the security is eventually redeemed, and the increase in the nominal annual yield need only be very small.

The issue of index-linked stock need not, of course, be confined to financing the budget deficit; it could also be used to refinance maturing debt, and this would further reduce the danger of unnecessary increases in interest rates because of irrational City fears. By issuing index-linked rather than conventional gilts the government, not the investor, would bear the risk of an increase in inflation. Not only would this help directly; the very fact that the government was willing to do this should itself help to damp down excessive inflationary expectations in the financial markets.

The second thing the government can do relates to another way in which a rational fiscal policy can be sabotaged by irrational City reactions. This concerns the foreign-exchange markets. If domestic or overseas holders of sterling take the view that a budget deficit, by way of a higher inflation rate, is likely to lead to a depreciation in the value of the pound, they will sell sterling (unless they are compensated for the increased exchange risk by a rise in interest rates). In the extreme case the currency, if it is floating, may fall a long way, risking the creation of a dangerous inflationary spiral. If it is fixed, it may be forced to devalue to a lower parity (as happened in 1967) or leave the fixed regime altogether (as happened in 1992). Unless devaluation is permitted because of a need to regain competitiveness – in which case it should take place anyway – this may be regarded as a serious objection to a rational fiscal policy, if such a policy requires a budget deficit that frightens the financial markets.

What the government can do about this is to finance some or all of its deficit – and indeed some of its maturing debt, if that should be thought necessary – by issuing bonds denominated in foreign currencies. Investors would have no fear of losing out if sterling were devalued in terms of dollars or Deutschemarks because their assets would be held in the form of dollars or Deutschemarks. There would then be little need to bribe them with higher interest rates. The corollary, of course, is that the government, rather than the investor, would bear the losses resulting from any devaluation, just as the government, not the investor, bears the risks of higher inflation when it issues index-linked rather than conventional gilts. But this is a perfectly sensible thing for the government to do if it takes the view that the currency will not be devalued; and the fact that it is willing to bear the exchange risk is in itself likely to be a powerful factor reassuring the financial markets. And if the government is wrong, and the currency is devalued, the once-for-all exchange loss must be seen in the light of the higher level of output and income that the policy has led to.

One further point needs to be made in this connection. The risks of adverse reactions in the foreign-exchange markets when a country adopts an expansionary fiscal policy are likely to be much reduced if other countries are doing the same. This certainly does not mean that Britain should not go it alone in running budget deficits when necessary; but it does mean that at a time of world recession the British government should do more than it has been doing to urge expansionary policies on the European Community and the Group of Seven. Britain took advantage neither of its hosting of the G7 economic summit in London in July 1991, nor of its presidency of the European Community during the second half of 1992, to press for this kind of coordinated expansionary action.

If it be accepted that a government should adopt a deliberately expansionary fiscal policy, if this is needed to avoid or cure a recession, the question then arises of which side of its accounts it should operate on. Should it cut taxes, or should it increase public expenditure?

There is no simple or universally valid answer to this question. Nevertheless, any discretionary fiscal policy employed to influence the level of demand in the economy in the short run must satisfy two basic requirements.

First, whatever measures are taken should be both *quick-acting* and *temporary*. It is no good choosing measures that take two or three years to start having an effect. Not only will they not help in the short run; by the time they impinge on effective demand this may (though, of course, it may not) already be rising at an adequate rate. By the same token, it is no good adopting measures that will go on adding to demand for years to come. What is needed is a stimulus that is withdrawn – or even self-liquidating – when the overall demand for goods and services has risen to match the economy's ability to supply them.

The second essential requirement is that changes in taxes or in public expenditure made in order to manage the level of demand in the short run should at best promote, and at worst not inhibit, the achievement of broader, longer-term economic and social objectives. The proportion of the GDP that takes the form of public rather than private expenditure is a matter of great importance, which should be determined by democratic debate and decision; only in the short run, and to a marginal extent, should it be influenced by the needs of demand management. The same is true of the structure of taxation, and particularly of the breakdown between direct taxes, which are progressive, and indirect taxes, which are usually regressive.

On the basis of these criteria it can be asserted with some confidence that major public-sector investment programmes are not suitable candidates for the task of short-term demand management. They are like supertankers: very slow to get under way, very difficult to stop when they are under way. Even trying simply to accelerate or slow down such programmes is likely to be disruptive and wasteful. Minor public works, however, are a completely different matter. There is no reason why every government department and every local authority should not keep a reserve list of useful projects that can be started at short notice and completed within six months or a year. The most casual observation of the contemporary British scene reveals that there is no shortage of roads that need mending, hospitals that need maintaining, school buildings that need repairing, council housing estates that need refurbishing or even replacing – the list is endless. Many of these projects would have their first impact on the construction industry, which can respond very quickly to increased demand; and there would be a further rapid expansionary effect not only on manufacturing industries that supply the construction industry, but on the economy as a whole (via the operation of the Keynesian multiplier discussed on page 16). Moreover, minor public works of this kind could be quickly scaled down as the slack in the economy was taken up by rising demand from the private sector.

On the tax side of the government's accounts, the requirements outlined above make it imperative that demand management should not involve cuts in the basic rate of income tax. Once income tax is cut, it is politically exceedingly difficult to put it up again. What happens instead, in the medium to longer run, is that (usually regressive) indirect taxes are increased, or that public expenditure is cut to an undesirable extent, or that a structural budget deficit is allowed to develop. (Indeed, all three things can happen together, as is attested by the experience of the last decade in both Britain and the United States, though this was the result not of attempts to manage the economy in an intelligent fashion, but of a determination to reduce income taxes on the better off, come hell or high water.) This does not necessarily mean that income tax has to be rejected altogether as a short-term regulator of effective demand; to impart a temporary stimulus to the economy the government could, for example, announce a once-for-all 10 per cent reduction in income tax *bills* for the coming year, or a one- or two-month tax holiday. Alternatively it could, for one or two years, raise tax thresholds by more than the inflation rate – if it was prepared to raise them by less than inflation for a year or two once economic recovery had taken place.

There is, however, one disadvantage of temporary tax cuts as a way of increasing effective demand: they may be saved rather than spent. 'Aha!' people may say to themselves. 'The government is temporarily cutting taxes, so it must be expecting a recession. Instead of spending this unexpected largesse, we'd better save it against a rainy day.' (They could conceivably save *more* than the tax cuts, so that the government's action will reduce effective demand rather than increase it.) This was particularly true in 1992–3, when the operation of 'debt deflation' meant that millions of households were cutting their spending in an attempt to reduce their debts (and, in many cases, to stave off repossession of their homes). Tax cuts in these circumstances would very often have been used to pay off debt rather than spent. For this reason a programme of quick-acting public-sector projects is likely to be more predictable in its effects.

All this is a far cry from what the British government was actually saying and doing as the recession of the early 1990s worsened. In late 1992 and early 1993 there was much ministerial talk not of reducing taxes but of increasing them. This might well be necessary in the medium term, but would be counter-productive at a time when the economy was still deep in recession. Perhaps this was pure rhetoric, designed to impress the financial markets. Actions speak louder than words. But actions pointed in the same perverse direction. Hospital wards were closed; school teachers were laid off; public libraries were axed; municipal swimming baths shut their doors. All this, according to the government, because 'the money isn't there'. Keynes had answered this idiocy in evidence he gave to the Macmillan Committee in 1930. 'We get into a vicious circle; we do nothing because we have not the money,' he said; 'but it is precisely because we do not do anything that we have not the money.' It is a pity that more than sixty years later this message needs to be relearned.

6

STRENGTHENING THE SUPPLY SIDE

Demand management is a necessary condition if the economy is to stay at full employment and enjoy a reasonable rate of growth. But it is not a sufficient condition. It is no good if the government, faced by high or rising unemployment, takes steps to increase effective demand and then finds that there is no adequate response on the supply side. If rising demand runs into capacity shortages because the capital stock is obsolete or inadequate, or because labour with the right qualifications and skills is simply not available, the result will not be rising output and rising employment but rising prices and rising imports. Accelerating inflation or a looming balance-of-payments crisis is likely to force the government to slam on the brakes, aborting the recovery, long before unemployment has been brought down to tolerable levels.

Mrs Thatcher's government took the view that problems of this kind would not arise provided that market forces were allowed to play their proper role. The matter would be dealt with in the way explained by nineteenth-century economic theory. If there were shortages of capacity, the profit motive would see to it that more capacity was installed. If skilled labour was in short supply, firms would train more skilled labour, and a rise in the wages of skilled labour would ensure that plenty of people came forward to seek training. A market economy, in which resources were allocated by the price mechanism, with a minimum of intervention from the centre – that was the answer.

As if the theory were not enough, there were also the facts. Ever since the end of the Second World War the market economies of the West and of Japan had been steadily (or fairly steadily) delivering rising living standards to their people. For a long time it was supposed that the centrally planned, or 'command', economies of the Soviet Union and Eastern Europe were doing the same. Speaking in 1957 of the prospects for peaceful economic competition with the United States, the Soviet leader Mr Khrushchev flatly declared, 'We shall bury you.' Coming from a nation with vast resources of every kind, which seemed to accord a proper priority to educating and training its people, which had the technology to put the first satellite into orbit and the first man into space, the claim did not seem unduly fanciful. But putting a man into space, it turned out, was a lot easier for a command economy than putting goods into the shops. The factories of the Soviet Union and its Eastern European neighbours churned out plenty of cement and plenty of steel, but somehow the cement failed to get turned into houses and the steel failed to get turned into consumer goods. By the late 1980s discontent with the inefficiency and corruption of the centrally planned economies had become acute, and by the early 1990s the system of central control was nearly everywhere in a state of collapse. If the communist countries themselves had come to acknowledge the superiority of a system based on market forces, who were Western politicians or economists to disagree? Mrs Thatcher knew, as always, that she had been right all along.

What Mrs Thatcher inherited in 1979, of course, was an economy very far removed from the centrally controlled communist model. To her, nevertheless, it appeared to be shackled by restrictions and regulations that inhibited the proper working of market forces and the efficient allocation of resources. (Thus foreign-exchange controls, which had been in force since 1939, were quickly abolished.) She also saw – and in this respect she probably had most of the nation with her – a trade union movement that had grown much too strong and arrogant. The Labour government had been unable to cope with the abuses of union power which disgraced the 'winter of discontent' in 1978–9, and which reinforced fears that had been growing since the late 1960s that the power of the unions was threatening to make the country ungovernable. A series of Acts of Parliament in the early 1980s soon put a stop to that. The legal immunities enjoyed by the unions were severely curtailed; secondary picketing was banned; secret ballots were required for union elections and for strike action. This legislation, aided by the rise in unemployment during the first half of the 1980s, helped to strengthen the role of market forces in areas where they were legitimate. A shift in the balance of power, particularly on the shop floor, made it easier for employers to reduce restrictive practices, eliminate over-manning and generally introduce changes that significantly raised productivity.

Another policy for extending the operation of market forces lay in the 'privatization' of the nationalized industries. This emerged as a major element of economic policy only in 1983, but was then pursued with almost evangelical fervour. By the time Mrs Thatcher resigned, about half the nationalized industries had been sold off, and plans to sell off most of the rest of them, including the coal industry and the railways, were in hand. Even the prisons were to be privatized.

Some privatizations, such as those of the aircraft and shipbuilding industries, made economic sense, since the building of ships and aircraft is an activity where competition is important and market forces have a crucial role. Other privatizations were far more questionable, seeming to be less a case of the introduction of market forces than of the application of inappropriate dogma. Many nationalized industries were 'natural monopolies', in which overhead costs are so great that competition makes no sense (imagine two sets of water mains or gas pipes or electricity cables or telephone lines running along every street and into every house). This is the main reason these industries were nationalized in the first place: if the technology of the industry is such that maximum efficiency calls for a single supplier, the single supplier had better be directly answerable to the community, in the form of the government, and not just to private shareholders concerned with profits and dividends. All that privatization of some of these industries has done is to turn public monopolies into private monopolies, and although these private monopolies are supposed to be regulated by government-appointed authorities, the efforts of these bodies to control the prices or curb the profits – and boardroom salaries – of these industries have in the main proved pretty feeble. Indeed, the proclaimed economic advantages, in terms of giving freer rein to market forces, of privatizing these industries are so spurious that it is difficult not to regard the strategy as having a political rather than an economic objective. This, some would say, was the creation of a large class of voters (those who bought shares in the newly privatized industries at the bargain-basement prices at which they were offered) who would never risk letting in another Labour government.

In addition to trade union reform and privatization, Mrs Thatcher had a third policy for strengthening the supply side of the economy: reductions in income tax, particularly on the higher-paid. People did not work hard enough, the argument went, or accept promotion, or take risks, or move to more productive jobs, because too large a slice of the extra income they would receive would go in tax. Therefore marginal income tax rates should be reduced, the burden being shifted to indirect taxes, such as Value Added Tax (which was raised from 8 per cent to 15 per cent in 1979 and to $17\frac{1}{2}$ per cent in 1991).

There would be little disagreement now that the marginal tax rates in operation in 1979 were too high. On the highest incomes the top rate was 83 per cent, and because there was a 15 per cent surcharge on investment (or unearned) income the highest marginal rate could be as high as 98 per cent. Too many people at the top of the income scale spent too much of their time avoiding these punitive tax rates, and too little of it getting on with their jobs. Whether the big cuts in income tax under Mrs Thatcher really had any significant effect in improving the supply side of the economy, however, seems doubtful. There is no convincing evidence that the 'substitution' effect of such tax cuts significantly outweighs the 'income' effect – i.e. that people, on balance, work harder because they now keep a larger slice of each extra pound they earn, rather than less hard because they do not need to earn so many pounds in order to enjoy the same post-tax income. Evidence from the United States, where similar big cuts in income tax took place under President Reagan, is also inconclusive. Thus although some entrepreneurs, executives and other key figures who determine the nation's destiny no doubt worked harder and took more risks, many probably did the opposite. More hours at the desk may have been a less frequent response than more hours on the golf course.

It is particularly hard to believe that the reductions in income tax in Britain in 1988 (see page 58) had any effect in promoting harder work or encouraging bolder entrepreneurial behaviour. In the budget that year Mr Lawson reduced the basic rate from 27 per cent to 25 per cent, and the top marginal rate from 60 per cent to 40 per cent. This top rate of 40 per cent was lower than in any other industrial country apart from Switzerland. If account is taken of state and local income taxes and employees' social security contributions (none of which applies in Britain on income taxed at 40 per cent), the top marginal rate in Germany was 56 per cent, France 62 per cent and Japan 76 per cent. Even in the United States (where the *federal* income tax is low) it was, on average, 46 per cent. This last round of tax cuts in Britain seemed to have less to do with improving the supply side of the economy than with rewarding those in the top 5 per cent of the income distribution.

At the opposite end of the income scale, motivations were assumed to be quite different (as J. K. Galbraith has remarked, the assumption seemed to be that the rich did not work because they were paid too little, while the poor did not work because they were paid too much). Mrs Thatcher's government took a series of steps to reduce the value of unemployment benefits in relation to wages: earnings-related unemployment benefits were abolished; unemployment benefits became taxable; and supplementary benefits (later called income support) were raised in line with prices, not earnings. If these measures were supposed to motivate the unemployed to equip themselves with new skills or move to parts of the country where work might be easier to find, they were singularly unsuccessful. Their main effect was to increase poverty among the bottom fifth of the population.

Any favourable effects that trade union reform, privatization and tax cuts may have had on Britain's ability to produce the goods and services that people at home and abroad want to buy seem to have been swamped by unfavourable developments of other kinds. Two are particularly important: the erosion of Britain's manufacturing base, and the failure to educate and train the labour force in the required skills.

Much has been heard about the improvement in manufacturing productivity in Britain during the 1980s. (Mr Lawson once incautiously described it as a 'miracle'.) It is true that during the earlier part of the period there was some narrowing of the gap between manufacturing productivity in Britain and some of its main competitors. But this was because productivity growth slowed down in other countries, not because it speeded up significantly in Britain, where it grew hardly any faster than it had in the 1960s and early 1970s (before the first oil shock). At the beginning of the 1990s it was still lower than in most other comparable countries.

Whatever happened to manufacturing *productivity*, what happened to manufacturing *production* was ominous. Between 1979 and 1981 manufacturing output fell by 15 per cent. Even in 1986 it was still about 5 per cent lower than it had been in 1979 – a seven-year period during which manufacturing output rose by 5 per cent in Germany, 15 per cent in the United States, and 25 per per cent in Japan. Britain's *imports* of manufactures, however, were almost 50 per cent higher in 1986 than they had been in 1979, a startling indication of the failure of the country's supply side to respond to rising demand. In 1983, for the first time in its history, Britain became a net importer of manufactured goods, and the gap between imports and exports of manufactures continued to grow until the onset of the recession in 1990–91. The huge current-account deficit of £22 billion in 1989 was overwhelmingly due to this gap between imports and exports of manufactured goods.

The government's indifference to what happened to manufacturing industry during the 1980s reflected an attitude of mind which had long characterized the British establishment. This was the idea (which Winston Churchill had castigated in 1925, when he wrote, 'I would rather see Finance less proud and Industry more content') that manufacturing did not really matter; that what Britain excelled at was providing financial services; and that that was where its future lay. (The dangerous complacency of this view was illustrated by a series of colossal losses in the banking and insurance sectors in the late 1980s and early 1990s.) A vicious circle of decline and neglect developed in the manufacturing sector. The fall in manufacturing output in 1979–81 – the result of inappropriately tight fiscal and monetary policies, and the overvalued exchange rate to which they contributed – led to the disappearance of more than a quarter of the nation's manufacturing capacity. Investment in manufacturing fell by a third between 1979 and 1982, and during the first half of the 1980s net investment in manufacturing (after allowing for depreciation) was actually *negative* – something regarded with grateful amazement by Britain's foreign competitors. This large fall in manufacturing investment and manufacturing capacity in turn made it impossible for output to respond to rising demand.

It is not going to be easy to restore or maintain full employment in Britain until substantial progress has been made in reversing the erosion of the manufacturing base, if only because it is not clear how the country could afford to pay for the level of imports that would be associated with a full employment level of output and income. The more competitive exchange rate established in the aftermath of Black Wednesday in September 1992 will help, provided this new competitiveness can be maintained, and not be rapidly whittled away by higher inflation. So, of course, will a revival in the world economy. But a great deal more investment in manufacturing industry is going to be needed, as well as more expenditure on research and development, to create the new products that people will want to buy, and the new processes that can turn them out at competitive prices. The hands-off attitude of the British government throughout the 1980s needs to be smartly reversed.

More can be done (as it is being done by the governments of many overseas competitors) to promote investment by the use of incentives, including – during recession – 'time-limited' incentives designed to bring investment expenditure forward. Much greater emphasis can be put, as it is in other countries, on the encouragement of research and development (Britain was the only Organization for Economic Cooperation and Development (OECD) country in which R & D expenditure fell, as a percentage of the GDP, in the 1980s). But the main incentive must come from an economic policy that avoids the roller-coaster ups and downs the country has suffered since 1979. When the home economy is allowed to plunge into recession, or the exchange rate is allowed to rise in a way that suddenly decimates the ability to compete in both export and domestic markets, manufacturing industry is devastated. Firms are closed down; plant and equipment are scrapped; management, design and sales teams are dispersed; skilled workers find themselves on the dole and, after a while, lose the motivation and attitudes needed to adapt to new job requirements. Perhaps demand recovers a few years later, but then it is too late: the capacity to produce has disappeared, and the goods in demand have to be imported from abroad.

The second area to which much more attention must be paid if Britain is to be able to supply the goods demanded in today's global marketplace, and to keep unemployment to a minimum, is that of education and training.

The main problem lies in *vocational*, rather than academic, education and training. Britain's record on this has never been particularly good, but since 1979 it has got much worse, mainly because of the government's faith in market forces, and its instinctive hostility to public expenditure. The argument went thus: if firms stood to gain, in terms of higher profits, from training more workers, they would train them. If they did not stand to gain, that just proved that more training was not needed. Unfortunately this piece of reasoning overlooks the fact that profit-maximizing firms will not incur costs in order to create benefits that will be enjoyed by others. Nobody expects individuals to spend money on providing street lighting, most of the benefit of which will go, free of charge, to others. Similarly, firms will be reluctant to spend money on training or retraining workers in modern skills if they fear – with good reason, to judge by British experience – that these workers will soon be poached by other firms which can offer more money because they have not themselves incurred the cost of providing any training. It is a sad and long-standing example of undue reliance on market forces leading to underprovision of an essential factor of production. To cope with this problem, the 1964–70 Labour government established a series of statutory industrial training boards, which imposed a training levy on firms not providing an adequate level of training themselves. With the sole exception of the board for the construction industry, all these boards were abolished by the post-1979 Conservative government.

On 16 November 1989 – more than ten years after the Conservative government took office – Mr Norman Fowler, Secretary of State for Employment, described the results of an extensive study commissioned by the government into the state of vocational training in Britain as 'mind-boggling'. Any comparison of Britain's training arrangements with those of other advanced countries is likely to confirm this view. Studies conducted in the later 1980s by the National Institute of Economic and Social Research, for example, showed that the much higher levels of productivity in German than in British factories owed an enormous amount to the much higher skill levels of German workers. Virtually all Germans who leave school at sixteen receive three years of compulsory vocational training, and two-thirds of them end up with an examined vocational qualification. These proportions, depending on the industry, are between five and ten times as high as are found in British factories. Similarly, something like seven times as many foremen in Germany as in Britain have acquired high technical and organizational qualifications. It is hardly surprising that the use of computer numerically controlled machinery is far greater in Germany, or that German factories are much more likely than British ones to be supplying the quality end of the market.

What Britain urgently needs, and has long needed, is a properly structured and adequately funded scheme for providing vocational education and training, leading to internationally recognized qualifications for all school-leavers who do not go on to higher or further education. This cannot be had – as British governments like to believe – on the cheap. The funding must be provided by the government: it is a good example of the kind of public expenditure, discussed on page 77, that is not capital expenditure but can yield very high rates of return. It is extraordinary that, whereas virtually all university students receive free tuition and a great many of them get government support for their maintenance, those who undergo vocational training have to finance much of the cost themselves. This helps to explain why the proportion of young people going to university has been rising rapidly (some would say too rapidly, particularly in view of the government's failure to fund this expansion properly), whereas the number receiving adequate vocational training remains lamentably small.

It is of paramount importance and urgency that Britain should build up a stronger manufacturing base and a better-educated and better-trained labour force if it is to prosper in the 1990s and beyond. It is no good increasing effective demand if there is no skilled labour and no manufacturing capacity available to satisfy it. But it is also no good training or retraining people in new skills if there are no jobs for them to do. Ensuring that there is an adequate level of effective demand remains the government's most important economic task.

7

THE INTERNATIONAL CONTEXT

As was observed in chapter 1, the current British recession is the worst suffered by any major OECD country in the last quarter-century. Moreover, it is not in any sense the consequence of the world recession of the early 1990s. Britain's recession started in the middle of 1990. Between the first half of 1990 and the first half of 1991 GDP fell by nearly 3 per cent, whereas for the twenty-four OECD countries, taken as a whole, GDP continued to grow over the period, albeit very slowly. Even in 1992 OECD output was probably about $1\frac{1}{2}$ per cent higher than in 1991, whereas in Britain there was a further decline of 1 per cent or so. World trade, too, continued to expand at a rate of 4–5 per cent in 1990 and 1991, and British exports of goods (though not of services) grew broadly in line with this, taking the two years as a whole. In short, although the world recession will make Britain's recovery more difficult, it played little or no part in creating the mess Britain has got itself into. Britain's recession was home-grown.

World recessions are so complex in their origins and so unpredictable in their workings that not even the most dedicated demand management by the OECD or Group of Seven countries could be expected to eliminate them altogether. It is clear, however, that during the quarter century or so since about 1970 these recessions have constituted more of a problem than they did during the previous quarter century. A general reason for this has been that in most Western countries, as in Britain, there has been a lower tolerance of inflation from the early 1970s onward than there had been before. Inflation, rather than unemployment, came to be seen as the great threat to the economic well-being of the mass of the people, and there was more support than there had been earlier for policies aimed at keeping inflation low, even at the expense of higher unemployment. And, particularly in Britain and the United States, this led to the rejection of Keynesian demand management.

Against this general background there were more specific reasons for the recessions of 1974–6 and 1980–83: the two oil shocks. Oil prices quadrupled between October 1973 and January 1974, and doubled between the beginning of 1979 and the beginning of 1980. These large and sudden increases had a direct deflationary effect on world trade and output, because people and businesses around the world now had to pay so much more for their oil that they had less left over to spend on other things. Moreover the oil-exporting countries whose incomes had now risen so enormously found, like any football pool winner, that in the short run there was no way to spend all this extra money. However, the jump in oil prices also had an inflationary effect, because it raised the price of petrol and, indeed, the price of all commodities made with (or of) oil. In order to prevent these oil-price increases from setting off an inflationary spiral, with wages and prices chasing each other upwards, Western governments adopted restrictive policies and, in particular, restrictive monetary policies. These restrictive policies were pursued more vigorously in some countries (such as Germany and Japan) than in others (such as Britain and Italy), and were in general pursued more vigorously after the second oil shock than after the first. Nevertheless, they were a substantial contributory factor to the recessions of both the mid-1970s and the early 1980s.

The world recession of the early 1990s was more complex in its origins, but two particular factors can perhaps be singled out. One was the excessive expansion of credit, especially in the English-speaking countries and Japan, in the later 1980s. The other was the reunification of Germany in 1990.

The excessive growth of credit in the United States, Britain and Japan in the later 1980s was itself, in a roundabout way, partly a consequence of the two oil shocks of the 1970s. The oil-exporting countries had deposited their hugely increased earnings in Western banks. These banks then lent the money to the middle-income oil-importing developing countries – particularly those in Latin America – whose growth rates were high and where rates of return looked good. These countries, in turn, were now able to afford to go on importing the oil they needed. Thus the OPEC surpluses were neatly recycled. Everybody congratulated themselves on how well market forces, operating internationally, had coped with the situation. Unfortunately, it all went sour. In August 1982 Mexico, the second biggest borrower of all (after Brazil), announced that it could no longer service its debt. Others followed. The banks, innocently believing that 'countries don't go bankrupt', had collectively (but in an uncoordinated way, not bothering to find out what other banks were doing) lent far more to these countries than they were ever likely to get back. Licking their badly burned fingers, they stopped lending abroad, and turned their attention to borrowers within their own borders. Any domestic property developer or fly-by-night business, it seemed, looked a better bet than a foreign government or parastatal organization.

This was one of the factors behind the rapid growth of bank lending within the United States, Britain and Japan in the mid to late 1980s. But a more general explanation lies in the ethos of the times, an ethos that both contributed to, and benefited from, the election of President Reagan in the United States and Mrs Thatcher in Britain. Market forces were best. Competition was king. Regulations and restrictions on the activities of economic agents, whether they be banks, or airlines, or media empires, or mining corporations were to be swept away. Banks and other financial institutions were to be free to lend as much as they liked, and, since it was assumed that the more they lent, the bigger the profits they would make, businesses and families were inveigled into borrowing more than made any sense, particularly (in Britain at least) for house purchase. In America the technique of the leveraged buy-out was perfected: a group of managers would buy out the equity in their company, stripping out and selling the profitable assets and financing their purchase by issuing high-yielding 'junk bonds'. The servicing of these junk bonds would be the first casualty of any fall in the company's cash flow resulting from a slowing down of the economy, and this would have a domino effect throughout the financial system. And so, towards the end of the decade, it proved.

Many of the loans made by the banks in the excitement of the mid to late 1980s were perfectly sound and well secured; but many were not. Much lending was for property development in one form or another, and the price of commercial property contains such a large subjective element that it can suffer big fluctuations. Many banks found that property companies to which they had lent money went bankrupt a lot more decisively than any developing country. Loans had to be written off, and banks became more wary about lending to any but the most blue-chip borrowers. This 'credit crunch' interacted with 'debt deflation' – the process whereby families and firms which had over-borrowed were forced to cut their expenditures in an endeavour to service their debt. This became more difficult as governments, in an attempt to curb the credit boom, raised interest rates. As incomes declined and interest rates rose, firms and individuals started to go bankrupt. Banks' balance sheets deteriorated, and they became even more reluctant to lend to anyone who looked in the least bit risky; and this reluctance to lend meant that even more businesses and individuals went bankrupt.

All this was more true of Britain, America and Japan, where the worship of market forces went to extremes in the 1980s, than it was of the economies of continental Europe. But in many of these countries a quite different factor played a part in creating and prolonging the recession of the early 1990s. This was the reunification of Germany.

When Germany was reunified in October 1990, 16 million East Germans were joined to 63 million West Germans whose productivity and real incomes were four times as high. If the 16 million were not to move west in search of higher living standards (and no one in the former West Germany was very keen on that), wages had to rise substantially in the east; and, strongly abetted by the West German trade unions, which had no wish to be subjected to low wage competition from their new compatriots, that is what occurred. But since most industry in the east was hopelessly obsolete and uncompetitive, particularly at these high wages, it seemed likely that workers in the east would simply lose their jobs and move west anyway. To forestall this, the German government started to finance infrastructure investment in the east, and to make large transfers of money, mainly in the form of measures to prevent widespread bankruptcies, and subsidies to housing, transport and pensions. These financial transfers should have been paid for by raising taxes, but the government, which perhaps for electoral reasons had much understated the costs that reunification would impose on citizens in western Germany, proved reluctant to do this. The Bundesbank, sniffing inflation in the air, started to push up short-term interest rates. These were already over 8 per cent – a high level by recent German standards (in 1987 and 1988 they had been around 4 per cent). Now they were pushed steadily upwards, with the aim of curbing the money supply and controlling inflation, to a level of nearly 10 per cent by mid-1992. They were still at this sort of level – there was a very small reduction in September 1992 – at the beginning of 1993. These high interest rates played a major part in precipitating a recession in Germany and, because they put a floor under interest rates in other ERM countries, they had a similar impact on most of the rest of Europe.

Of the two particular factors singled out above as having helped to create the current world recession, one – the excessive expansion of credit in the United States, Britain and Japan – could have been avoided and, if the lesson has been learned, will be avoided in future. The other – the effect on German interest rates of reunification – while historically unique in itself, raises some disturbing questions. How can Britain, or any other European country, create or maintain full employment if this calls for a monetary policy that is inconsistent with the policy of the Bundesbank? If interest rates throughout Europe are determined largely by German central bankers with the German inflation rate as virtually their sole preoccupation, what scope is there for a rational macroeconomic policy in other European countries? More specifically, if the Bundesbank keeps interest rates high until the German inflation rate (running at around 4 per cent in 1991 and 1992) comes down to no more than 1 or 2 per cent, does this not presage a prolonged recession in the rest of Europe? And even if this problem is somehow dealt with this time round, may it not all happen again at some point in the future?

Although these are legitimate concerns, they should not be

exaggerated, nor should they be used as an excuse for inaction. A number of points need to be borne in mind.

First, fiscal policy is a powerful weapon (more powerful than monetary policy) for getting an economy out of recession. There is no reason why fiscal policy in Britain or other European countries should be constrained by what the Bundesbank decides about short-term interest rates in Germany. Quick-acting, temporary increases in public expenditure or reductions in taxation, designed to raise the level of demand, can be put in hand regardless of the level of interest rates in either Germany or Britain.

Secondly, the argument that private investment cannot recover while short-term interest rates are high needs to be treated with considerable scepticism. For one thing, short-term interest rates are less relevant to investment decisions than long-term interest rates, and the two can diverge markedly. Throughout 1992, for example, when German short-term interest rates averaged about $9\frac{1}{2}$ per cent, long-term rates averaged about $7\frac{3}{4}$ per cent. During 1990, when British short-term rates averaged almost 15 per cent, long-term rates averaged only about $11\frac{1}{2}$ per cent. More important, however, is that in most investment decisions the level of interest rates is only one of several factors to be considered. Carrying more weight are the prospects for sales and profits. Government action to expand the economy, or keep it operating at a high level, will boost investment even if interest rates are high. If the outlook is for continuing or worsening recession, on the other hand, even low interest rates may have little effect in stimulating investment.

Thirdly, the need to align short-term interest rates with those set by the Bundesbank is much less pressing if a country is outside the European Monetary System. A country has far more control over its own monetary policy if the exchange rate is floating than if it is fixed: that is why monetarist economists were so opposed to Britain's entry into the ERM in October 1990, and so relieved by its departure in September 1992. Strictly speaking, even with a floating pound, British interest rates could be lower than German ones only if the foreign exchange markets thought that the pound had floated down too far, and was likely to appreciate against the Deutschemark, thus compensating for the lower interest yield. But foreign exchange markets are so irrational and unpredictable that in practice this condition will not necessarily be fulfilled. It is symptomatic of this unpredictability that when the pound was floated in September 1992 some of those who had thought, correctly, that entry into the ERM in October 1990 would permit a reduction in British interest rates now believed, logically enough, that they would have to be raised in order to prevent the pound falling too far, and setting off an inflationary spiral. In the event, they were proved wrong, at any rate in the short run: base rates in Britain were brought down from 10 per cent to 7 per cent over the next two months (and later to 6 per cent), while the most relevant German interest rate (the Lombard rate) stayed at $9\frac{1}{2}$ per cent. Sterling, in the meantime, stabilized at what seemed the reasonable rate of DM 2.40–DM 2.50. But how long this combination of low interest rates and satisfactory exchange rates was sustainable remained unclear.

Finally, if more tentatively, it might be observed that not even the Bundesbank can remain completely impervious to the effects of its monetary stance on output and employment within Germany itself. If high interest rates have depressing effects on consumption and investment in Germany, or cause other ERM countries to devalue or leave the ERM altogether, thus reducing the competitiveness of German industry, pressures for monetary relaxation within Germany itself are bound to grow. Deep in the subconscious of the Bundesbank may be the hyperinflation that destroyed the German middle classes in the early 1920s, but it was the heavy unemployment of the early 1930s that actually brought Hitler to power in 1933. A severe recession in Germany might erode support for transfers to the eastern part of the country, with consequences for living standards and employment there that could create serious political and social problems.

The discussion in the last few pages relates to the situation in the early 1990s. Britain has had plenty of scope to increase demand in order to avoid, or at the very least emerge from, the serious recession it has fallen into, and this scope was enlarged by its departure from the Exchange Rate Mechanism in September 1992.

By the end of the decade, however, things may be very different. Under the provisions of the Maastricht Treaty, signed by the twelve members of the European Community in December 1991, the third stage of the move to economic and monetary union – the creation of a single European currency – is to come into force by 1 January 1999 at the latest. Whether this will ever really happen is something nobody can know. There are deep divisions in Europe over the Maastricht Treaty. The Danes rejected it, by a margin of 50.7 to 49.3 per cent, in a referendum in June 1992 (though this outcome was reversed in a second referendum a year later); the French accepted it, by a margin of 51 to 49 per cent, in a referendum in September. Stage Three cannot in any case come into force until certain 'convergence criteria' are met: a majority of EC countries must have achieved very similar inflation rates, interest rates, budgetary positions, etc. Even if Stage Three does come into operation at the beginning of 1999, Britain does not have to be involved: at Maastricht it negotiated a special protocol, permitting it to opt out of the move to a single currency if it wished.

Nevertheless, if Europe is to move towards closer economic and political union – as presaged by the coming into operation of the single European market at the beginning of 1993 – the existence of eleven different currencies is going to look increasingly anomalous. And if the rest of the European Community adopts a single currency, the pressures on Britain to do the same are likely to be intense. The implications of such a move for the conduct of economic policy in Britain would be substantial. Two in particular are of major importance.

If Europe were to have a single currency, it would have to be issued by a single European central bank. Although Britain would be represented on the board of this institution, and would no doubt have some influence on its decisions, the country would effectively, and permanently, lose control of its own monetary policy. Decisions about targets for the growth of the money supply, and the interest rates needed to achieve them, would presumably be taken by some kind of weighted majority voting. If these decisions happened not to suit British circumstances, that would be just too bad.

Of crucial importance is the fact that the European Central Bank (ECB) would clearly be an independent one. It would be like the Bundesbank or the Federal Reserve Board in the United States (completely independent of government) and not like the Bank of England, whose policies are ultimately determined by the government of the day. Those who think that a low inflation rate is the only thing a central bank should be concerned with, and that the best way to achieve low inflation is to keep tight control of the money supply, either directly or by appropriate manipulation of interest rates, will welcome the prospect of an independent ECB. In Britain there are already strong pressures for the Bank of England to be made independent (as is in any case required by Stage Two of the move to economic and monetary union). But if (for reasons argued at length in earlier chapters) one takes the opposite view – that low inflation is only one of the objectives of economic policy, and that all the instruments available to the government should be used in a coordinated way to target all these objectives – then the prospect of an independent European Central Bank, whose only remit is to minimize the inflation rate, is a thoroughly alarming one.

The introduction of a single European currency would not remove individual countries' powers to conduct their own fiscal policies, in the way that it would eliminate their ability to conduct independent monetary policies. In principle, an individual country could still adopt an expansionary fiscal policy if it wanted to stimulate demand, or to offset what it regarded as an undesirably tight monetary policy on the part of the ECB. But in practice there might be difficulties. Among the 'convergence criteria', for example, the Maastricht Treaty lays down that budget deficits should not exceed 3 per cent of GDP, and the National Debt should not exceed 60 per cent of GDP; and these requirements – entirely arbitrary though they are – could constrain an independent fiscal policy in times of recession. Moreover, there is likely to be an increasing harmonization of tax rates throughout the Community in order to create a level competitive playing field, and this too might limit individual governments' freedom of action on the fiscal front. This point can be exaggerated, as the existence of a variety of tax and expenditure regimes in different American states makes clear, but it is not baseless.

The second major implication of the introduction of a single European currency is simple but far-reaching. Individual countries could no longer devalue, or revalue, their currencies. (Europe as a whole could, of course, still devalue or revalue the ECU – or whatever its currency was called – against the dollar or the yen.) This means that if an individual country became less competitive because its money wages rose faster, or its productivity more slowly, than elsewhere in Europe, it would not be able to restore its competitive position by changing its exchange rate. Devaluation does not, of course, provide a permanent cure for loss of competitiveness, because it is unlikely to change the factors, such as excessive wage increases or a sluggish growth of productivity, that have caused the loss of competitiveness in the first place. But it is a simple, overnight way of restoring lost competitiveness at a particular time – far simpler than the alternative, which is a reduction in money wages. If the exchange-rate weapon were removed, a lack of competitiveness would become much more difficult to remedy.

Such a lack of competitiveness would no longer lead, as it has so often in Britain, to a balance-of-payments deficit. There can be no balance-of-payments deficit within a single currency area: the United States may sometimes have balance-of-payments problems, but Texas and Massachusetts do not. Instead, the problem created by a lack of competitiveness would take a different form. Unless costs could be reduced, or productivity increased, output and employment would fall. Unless there was emigration, unemployment would rise, and high unemployment and a depressed level of income might become chronic.

An analogy can be drawn between the position Britain (like some other countries, particularly on the geographical periphery of Europe) might find itself in if there were a single European currency, and the position that Scotland and Wales are in within Britain itself. Throughout much of the twentieth century Scotland and Wales have had higher unemployment and lower levels of per capita income than the Midlands and the south of England. There have been various reasons for this: a relatively high proportion of older and declining industries; a lack of competitiveness because lower productivity was not fully offset by lower wages, as economists with a naïve faith in the working of market forces would expect (many wage rates being nationally negotiated); and, in general, the disadvantages of being at a distance from the faster-growing areas of the country, where factors like a pool of skilled labour, and close proximity to markets, suppliers, sub-contractors, etc., provide a more attractive environment for new and expanding firms. These competitive disadvantages could not be overcome by Scottish or Welsh devaluation because (whatever the differences in the design of their pound coins) England, Scotland and Wales share a common currency.

The same difficulties could confront whole countries in the event of the adoption of a single European currency. Britain, as a country located on the edge of Europe, and one in which wages have historically tended to rise faster than some of its neighbours', and productivity rather more slowly, could be particularly at risk (though this risk might be moderated if Britain managed to stay opted out of the Maastricht Treaty's social chapter). Moreover, these difficulties would be greater than those which exist within the British Isles. For within individual countries there are powerful equilibrating mechanisms at work that moderate regional disparities. These would not be at work within a European Community that had a single currency.

One of these equilibrating mechanisms is simply the mobility of labour. A common language and a common culture make migration from high- to low-unemployment areas within Britain a fairly straightforward proposition – as it is within the US. Moving from Britain to some other European country in search of work would be a more formidable undertaking.

Much more important is the role of the government. In a unitary state like Britain (and, though to a lesser extent, in a federal state like the US) the activities of central government have a major impact on the regional pattern of output, incomes and employment. In Britain social security benefits and rates of direct and indirect tax are the same in all parts of the country. Resources will therefore be channelled automatically from prosperous areas, where incomes are high and unemployment low, to depressed areas, where incomes are low and unemployment high. Similarly, because standards of education and health care are supposed to be the same throughout the country, teachers and health-service workers have jobs and spend money even in areas where the private sector is at its most depressed. They also provide income in kind, in the form of free or subsidized education and medical treatment, that is fairly equally distributed across the country. Grants from central to local government which help to finance a variety of other public services are another factor that reduces regional disparities. In addition to this, throughout most of the post-war period specific regional subsidies and incentives of various kinds have been provided by the government with the aim of stimulating the growth and development of the more depressed areas.

All this is possible only because of the size of central government budgets – typically 40–45 per cent of GDP in advanced industrial countries that are unitary states, and 20–25 per cent in federations (which often have explicit fiscal equalization schemes). This compares with a European Community budget that is currently 1.2 per cent of GDP. Almost two-thirds of this goes on the Common Agricultural Policy, whose impact on regional inequalities is, if anything, perverse (of the ten European Community countries in the mid-1980s, for example, Denmark had the highest per capita income, yet received the second highest per capita subsidies from the CAP). Less than a fifth of the budget is specifically designated to help regions within the Community that have particularly low incomes or high unemployment. The figure of 1.2 per cent of GDP is in sharp contrast to the figure of $7\frac{1}{2}$–10 per cent which an expert group, set up by the European Commission under the chairmanship of Sir Donald MacDougall, concluded in 1977 would be necessary if European monetary union were to avoid unacceptable disparities in productivity and living standards in different parts of the Community. The subsequent accession of Greece, Spain and Portugal might require that estimate to be raised. But present plans are for an increase to no more than about 1.3 per cent by the later 1990s.

In the world depicted by classical economic theory and much contemporary economic literature the problems outlined in the last few paragraphs would not exist. Market forces would solve them. Britain could not become a high-unemployment, low-income region of Europe if there were a single European currency, because money wages in Britain would fall until Britain became fully competitive. But the world does not work like this, as the existence of high-unemployment, low-income regions within Britain clearly attests. And this is in spite of the operation of powerful equilibrating forces within Britain that would be largely absent in a Europe that had a single currency. It is possible that the creation of a single European currency would promote changes in institutional, particularly wage-setting, behaviour in Britain which would reduce the dangers discussed above. But although there might be some such effect, the response within the countries which joined the Exchange Rate Mechanism upon its inception in 1979 provides only limited grounds for optimism.

The severe constraints on British economic policy discussed in the last few pages belong in the future, when (or if) Europe has a single currency. They do not exist today. There have been no good reasons for allowing Britain to slide into recession, or for refusing to take appropriate action to get out of it. (Britain could have learned something from Japan, which responded to incipient recession by adopting expansionary fiscal measures – mainly increases in public investment – in August 1992, and again in April 1993.)

It is, of course, true that Britain has a very open economy. Exports of goods and services account for between a quarter and a third of Britain's GDP. The prices of its imports of primary products are determined by world supply and demand. There are no controls on capital movements to or from the rest of the world. There are no controls on the flow of people, or of goods and services, between Britain and the rest of the European Community. The economic situation in Britain is bound to be affected by developments abroad on which it has little or no influence. But all this should be regarded not as a reason for Britain to throw up its hands and say that nothing can be done. It should be regarded as a reason for using its membership of both the European Community and the Group of Seven to play a constructive role in promoting saner economic policies in the world of the mid to late 1990s than have been in evidence over the past decade and a half.

One of the main things Britain should do is to press for proper use to be made again of the annual economic summits of the Group of Seven industrial countries. In the later 1970s these were serious affairs. The leaders of these countries recognized that the world economy is now so interdependent that it makes little sense for the major nations to take unilateral decisions, without regard to the effects these decisions may have on other countries, or the way in which they may in turn react. Non-cooperative behaviour of this kind is almost bound to lead to a less than optimal outcome for all concerned. Instead, the leaders of the main countries should seek agreement on policies which are likely to improve the position of all of them.

The best example of the kind of policy coordination required is perhaps that of the G7 summit meeting held in Bonn in July 1978. At that time the world needed expansionary measures to boost the weak recovery from the recession induced by the 1973–4 oil shock. Most countries were reluctant to take such measures unilaterally, partly because of the likely effects on their balance of payments (their imports would rise but their exports would not). But a coordinated expansion would not only mini-mize the balance-of-payments risks to each country, but could give a general fillip to business confidence around the world. Accordingly, most of the G7 countries agreed to provide an extra boost to demand, mainly through the use of fiscal policy. Various other appropriate measures were also agreed, notably an increase in internal American oil prices to the world level within two years in order to reduce the high US level of oil imports. Like this one, several of the measures the leaders agreed to were likely to be unpopular back home, and would probably not have been adopted if it had been left to each of them individually. But, in an informal atmosphere of mutual urging and mutual concession, a certain amount of boldness prevailed, and a satisfactory package emerged. It was a positive-sum game. The whole, as the British Prime Minister James Callaghan remarked at the time, was greater than the sum of the parts.

Any idea of reaching this kind of agreement on the best way to stimulate the international economy was anathema to most of the leaders who took command at the beginning of the 1980s, particularly President Reagan and Mrs Thatcher. These two did not believe in managing their own economies, which should, in their view, be left to the benign influence of market forces. Any attempt to manage the world economy was obviously even further off the agenda. But in the early 1990s, now that a new generation has taken over in America and some of the extremes of Thatcherism appear to have been abandoned in Britain, there is some hope of getting back to the original Group of Seven summits. Instead of the kind of public-relations jamborees they became in the 1980s, designed to do little more than present world leaders in a flattering light to their domestic television audiences, they should again become occasions for informal but serious discussion and decision-making by the people at the very top. A useful first step would be to set up a permanent, high-powered G7 secretariat.

The main item on the next summit agenda should be the task of getting world growth going again, and unemployment down to acceptable levels. Subsequent summits should agree on policies to keep the world economy growing, and avoiding developments that might once again plunge it into recession.

A specific issue that needs to be addressed is exchange-rate regimes. The single European currency discussed earlier would have the characteristics of a system of irrevocably fixed exchange rates within Europe. If such a single currency is rejected as undesirable or impractical, at any rate in the foreseeable future, it will probably pay Europe, particularly now that a single market has been established, to persist with the existing Exchange Rate Mechanism or something very like it. Mr John Major has talked of the need for a fundamental rethink of the way the ERM operates, but his comments must be seen in the light of Britain's inability to sustain the value of the pound at the level Mr Major originally chose for it. There were no realignments within the ERM between early 1987 and September 1992, and the particular difficulties raised by German reunification are unlikely to recur. Whatever the arrangements within Europe, however, there will still remain the problem of the relationship between the European currencies, taken as a whole, and the world's other two main currencies, the dollar and the yen.

There is an intrinsic difficulty here. Foreign trade is much less important to the United States and Japan than it is to individual European countries (though the differences are less marked for the European Community taken as a whole). Exports account for less than 10 per cent of the US GDP and less than 15 per cent of Japan's. For individual European countries they often represent 25–35 per cent of GDP. Thus the economic gaze of governments in the US and Japan is more inward-looking than it is in Europe, and their attitude towards the external value of their currencies sometimes approaches indifference, particularly in the US. Other countries, however, cannot afford to be indifferent to what happens to the yen, with its effects on the competitiveness of Japanese exports, and even less to what happens to the dollar, still much the most important world currency.

This point is illustrated by the recent history of the dollar. Between 1980 and 1985 its 'effective' (or trade-weighted) exchange rate rose by 50 per cent. This was mainly the consequence of the combination of President Reagan's lax fiscal policy and the Federal Reserve Board's tight monetary policy, neither of which was adopted with the interests of other countries much in mind. Yet the rise in the dollar had disruptive effects all around the world. Developing countries found their debts much more expensive to service, because these had mainly been contracted in dollars and at variable rates of interest, both of which now went sky-high. The industrial countries found their imports of dollar-denominated primary products more expensive. Much of American industry, rendered uncompetitive by the exchange rates of the mid-1980s, suffered severe damage, and this strengthened the protectionist lobby in Washington. Equally disruptive, in different ways, was the fall in the dollar during the second half of the decade. This was so precipitous that by 1990 the dollar's external value was actually 15 per cent lower than it had been in 1980.

These large swings in exchange rates (a counterpart of the rise and fall in the dollar had been the fall and rise of the Deutschemark and, to a lesser extent, the yen) were the consequence of leaving them to be determined by supply and demand, with a minimum of government or central bank intervention. In this sphere, as in others, market forces had entirely failed to deliver the optimal outcome that had been predicted by economists such as Milton Friedman and Harry Johnson and politicians such as Mrs Thatcher. The argument that a floating exchange-rate regime would generate the right pattern of exchange rates had clearly been disproved. If the average 1980 rate of DM 1.82 to the dollar was right, the average 1985 rate of DM 2.94 must be wrong (particularly since inflation was considerably lower in Germany than in the US over the period). And if DM 2.94 was right in 1985, the average 1990 rate of DM 1.62 had to be wrong.

However, the fact that the floating exchange-rate regime to which the world moved in the early 1970s has experienced large and damaging swings does not mean that there is any realistic prospect of moving back to something like the Bretton Woods fixed exchange-rate regime that it replaced. That regime, which required countries to keep their currencies within 1 per cent of their central exchange rate against the dollar, had been unable to cope with the divergence of inflation rates in different countries in the 1960s, or the increasing freedom of capital movements. As the recent history of the ERM illustrates, the difficulties of operating a fixed exchange-rate regime even for the currencies of a group of countries which are bound together in an economic community can be formidable. It is unlikely that such a regime could easily include the currencies of countries in very different circumstances, such as the United States and Japan.

Perhaps the answer lies somewhere between the more or less free floating that has determined the value of the dollar and the yen for most of the past twenty years and the fixed exchange-rate regime that has operated in Europe since 1979. The ERM band of $2\frac{1}{4}$ per cent each side of a central rate would be too narrow to be sustainable in a regime that incorporated the dollar and the yen. On the other hand, a range of, say, 10 per cent each side of a central rate would probably be too wide, since it might – depending on the technical characteristics of the system – permit two individual currencies to move against each other by as much as 40 per cent. Such a movement would be nearly as big as some of the swings in the 1980s. A band of 5 per cent each side of a central rate might be a reasonable aim. Currencies would be kept within these limits by a combination of central bank intervention in the foreign-exchange markets and appropriate changes in monetary policy.

There is, however, a problem with any fixed exchange-rate regime: in certain circumstances it presents currency speculators with a pretty safe one-way bet. Sterling's experience in September 1992 is a case in point. Under the ERM rules the Bank of England was committed to buying (with temporary assistance from other ERM central banks) unlimited amounts of sterling to prevent its rate from falling below DM 2.778. Speculators could – and, with much talk of realignment in the air, did – sell billions of pounds to the Bank of England in exchange for Deutschemarks at this rate. They reasoned that, at worst, the pound's value would be held, and they would have lost nothing more than transaction costs. But if the Bank of England ran out of foreign exchange, or the government lost its nerve, the pound would be devalued and they would make a killing. In the event, many did.

The devaluation of the pound forced by speculation in September 1992 made perfectly good economic sense: the pound was overvalued. But speculation is not always so benign. Later that month, and on various occasions in subsequent months, speculation nearly forced the devaluation of the French franc as well. This would not have made economic sense: France had a lower inflation rate than Germany and a much stronger balance-of-payments position, and on fundamentals the franc was, if anything, undervalued rather than overvalued against the Deutschemark. The franc–Deutschemark link was held, at any rate well into 1993; but this was not for want of speculators trying to bust it.

There is no simple answer to the problem of speculators taking key economic relationships out of the hands of governments and central banks. Prime Ministers and central bank governors can make solemn pledges to maintain a particular exchange rate, but speculators who have disbelieved them have grown rich. To discourage speculators from borrowing and selling billions when they guess that devaluation is only days away, central banks can force up overnight interest rates to several hundred per cent, but this may not work either. Sweden raised overnight rates to 500 per cent to defend the krona in September 1992, but two months later similar tactics failed, and after $25 billion flowed out of the country in a matter of days it was forced to devalue. Nevertheless, it is becoming increasingly widely recognized that huge unrestricted capital flows between one currency and another in the pursuit of private profit can play havoc with rational economic policymaking, and that it is in the interests of all the major countries to impose some regulation on them. It should be possible for the Group of Seven countries to devise a system of penal taxes on short-term gains from operations of the big banks and other dealers which are undertaken solely in the hope of making money by betting on, and helping to bring about, changes in exchange rates. It should not, in principle, be difficult to distinguish the making of such short-term gains from the legitimate activities of investment trusts, insurance companies, pension funds, etc., whose job includes anticipating changes in exchange rates, like changes in many other variables, in making investment decisions.

Whatever new arrangements are worked out in the longer term about exchange rates, the immediate task of the Group of Seven must be to get back to low unemployment and a respectable rate of growth. If this can be achieved by the G7, which accounts for nearly two-thirds of global output, the rest of the world will be pulled along in its wake. If greater weight is attached to achieving full employment and faster growth there might, to be sure, emerge a problem of higher inflation, but the arguments put forward in chapter 3 suggest that, to paraphrase Mr Norman Lamont, that might be a price well worth paying. It is also true that different governments and different central banks may have different, and even conflicting, priorities. Life, it can safely be assumed, will never be easy for policymakers. But it is time they made a more constructive attempt to tackle these economic problems. That, after all, is one of the things we pay them for.

8

WHAT NOW?

At the beginning of 1993 some 3 million people in Britain – more than 10 per cent of the labour force – were unemployed. The other main industrial countries were in recession as well, but Britain's recession had started earlier than most, and gone deeper than any. More than most, too, Britain's recession was the culmination of a decade and a half of hands-off economic policies. According to the philosophy of monetarism, which began to have a major impact on economic policy in Britain in the mid-1970s, government action could have little effect on real variables, such as output and employment, and such effect as it did have would be short-lived and damaging. So demand management – the approach to policymaking followed in Britain since the war – was out: practised half-heartedly during the later days of the 1974–9 Labour government, jettisoned altogether by Mrs Thatcher in 1979. Instead, the budget was to be brought into rough balance and kept there, and the money supply was to be made to grow at a slow and steady pace. This would create a low or zero inflation rate and a stable, predictable environment for private-sector decision-makers. Market forces would be able to fulfil their function of promoting an efficient, prosperous, growing economy.

Unfortunately, the economy is not self-stabilizing, and if the government follows simple rules of thumb that assume that it is, there is likely to be trouble. There will be recessions (as in the early 1980s), inflationary booms (as in the late 1980s) and more recessions (as in the early 1990s). The fact is that the economy needs to be managed. If it has been allowed to plunge into recession, then, as Keynes argued in the *General Theory*, the government must step in and increase effective demand.

Reductions in interest rates are a weak and unreliable way of doing this: at a time of recession, the fact that businesses can borrow more cheaply in order to invest does not necessarily mean that they will want to do so. A better approach is an expansionary fiscal policy. What is called for are increases in government spending, or cuts in taxation, which will act quickly to increase demand, but which can be phased out or reversed as the economy comes back to full employment. This expansionary fiscal policy will lead, in the short run, to a bigger budget deficit than would occur automatically in a recession, but there is nothing wrong with that. The extra cost of servicing the National Debt that this deficit will lead to will be small in relation to the rise in output and incomes that it stimulates. There is no reason why the ratio of National Debt to GDP should necessarily rise. If there is an unjustifiable structural deficit in the government's accounts – meaning that the budget is still in deficit when the economy is once again operating at full employment – this will have to be tackled. In the Britain of the 1990s, where, it can be argued, public expenditure has been squeezed to such an extent that it threatens many of the decencies of life in a civilized society, taxes will have to be increased. But that is for the future. Tax increases make no sense at a time of recession.

What is needed now is a fiscal policy which increases demand, not one which reduces it. Such a policy must be pursued as vigorously as circumstances permit. Unfortunately, Britain's present circumstances are much less favourable than could be wished. The free market, monetarist policies pursued by Mrs Thatcher's government after 1979, based on a dogmatic and exaggerated faith in the virtues of liberalization, privatization and deregulation, have led to the emergence of three serious structural imbalances. These restrict the government's ability to bring the economy back to full employment simply by the use of an expansionary fiscal policy. One of these structural imbalances lies in the 'skills deficit' – the lack of skilled labour in relation to the demand for it. A second lies in the current account of the balance of payments. The third lies in the relationship between consumption and investment.

The skills deficit is the consequence of the belief that somehow or other market forces will see to it that suitably trained and educated labour will be forthcoming in response to demand for it. Britain has always been prone to this misguided belief, but after 1979 it became an unchallengeable article of faith. The lack of properly structured and adequately funded vocational education and training schemes has cost Britain dear, and will cost it even dearer in future unless urgent steps are taken to put it right. Although this is primarily a matter of vocational training, mismatches between the demand and supply of skills apply to academic qualifications as well. (At the beginning of 1993, in the depths of recession, British pharmaceutical companies in south-east England – world leaders in the field – were reporting difficulties in recruiting enough staff with A-level and graduate qualifications in chemistry to permit future expansion.) Unless the government starts to take the whole business of education and training a lot more seriously, it will be difficult for an expansionary fiscal policy, by itself, to bring the economy back to full employment.

Mr Nigel Lawson, when Chancellor of the Exchequer, took a relaxed view of the second structural imbalance identified above – Britain's chronic current-account deficit. He claimed that, provided it was the counterpart not of a government budget deficit but of a private-sector deficit (as was the case in 1988 and 1989), there was no problem, since a private-sector deficit (unlike a government deficit) eventually has to be reversed. If businesses and families chose to borrow in order to spend more than their income, that was their affair, and if the money they borrowed happened to be spent mainly on imported goods, that was their affair too. But this hands-off approach (inspired by a refinement of monetarism known as the rational expectations hypothesis) makes sense only if business and household borrowers know what they are doing – i.e. have realistic and mutually consistent plans for repaying the debt they are incurring. The history of business bankruptcies and house repossessions in the early 1990s shows what a naïve belief this is.

There is a cyclical element in the balance of payments that is related – as is the cyclical element in the government budget – to fluctuations in the economy itself. When the economy booms the current account tends to go into deficit, because imports rise without there being any reason for exports to do the same. Correspondingly, when the economy moves into recession the current account will improve, because imports will fall, and manufacturers may try harder to export. What is disturbing about the contemporary British case is that this cyclical pattern has been superimposed on a worsening trend – a trend that is only partly accounted for by the decline in North Sea oil's contribution to the balance of payments since the mid-1980s. The current-account deficit in the boom year 1989 was £22 billion; in the comparable boom year 1979 – well before North Sea oil was making its maximum contribution to the balance of payments – the current account was in virtual balance. Between 1981, the low point (in terms of output) of the previous recession, and 1992, the low point so far of the present recession, the volume of exports of manufactured goods rose by 75 per cent, while the volume of manufactured imports rose by 125 per cent. The consequence of this worsening trend is that even in the recession year 1992 there was a current-account deficit of £12 billion.

Any economic recovery after 1993, therefore, will start off with a current-account deficit of over 2 per cent of GDP. With the exception of the unique circumstances following the first oil shock, which affected all oil-importing countries, there is no precedent for this state of affairs. Thus a conventional fiscal expansion, taking the form of tax cuts or public expenditure increases which led to higher imports but little change in exports, would take the country into uncharted waters. This is particularly true now that Britain's manufacturing capacity has been so seriously eroded by the two recessions the country has suffered since 1979. In the short run, at least, a large part of any increase in effective demand, especially if it took the form of a rise in consumers' expenditure, would have to be met from abroad. A current-account deficit that looked like rising to 4 or 5 per cent of GDP might put severe downward pressure on sterling, and threaten to set off a spiral of rising inflation and falling exchange rate. This would have to be stopped by an increase in interest rates and a deflationary U-turn on fiscal policy which would certainly abort any recovery and might turn recession into slump.

What is needed ideally, therefore, is a recovery led by a growth of exports. This would obviously be easier if the rest of the world started to recover from recession, but although Britain, both within the European Community and as a member of the Group of Seven, should have been taking a much more active role in urging other governments to adopt expansionary measures, there is nothing it can do about it directly. In the meantime, monetary policy must be used to keep the nominal exchange rate at the sort of competitive level to which it fell in September 1992, and everything possible must be done to prevent this competitive edge from being eroded by rising wage costs. Advantage should be taken of the recession to reform wage-bargaining procedures and, in particular, to get broad agreement between government, employers and unions on the average rise in money wages that the economy can afford if it is to keep inflation low and the balance of payments on an improving trend. This, much more than the control of the money supply by the central bank, is the approach that has given countries such as Germany and Japan low inflation and a healthy balance of payments throughout most of the post-war period. It is high time Britain took a leaf out of that particular book.

Just as the structural imbalance which has arisen between exports and imports needs to be put right, so does the structural imbalance which has developed between consumption and investment. Over the past decade or so consumption in Britain has risen considerably faster than production. Consumers' expenditure accounted for 59 per cent of the GDP in 1979 but 65 per cent in 1989. This large rise in the ratio of consumption to output was mainly made possible by the deterioration in the balance of payments over the period. The share of consumption in GDP was still 65 per cent in 1991 (the last year for which full figures are available). This compared with 63 per cent in Italy, 61 per cent in France, 57 per cent in Japan and 55 per cent in Germany. Only in the United States, among the major countries, was it higher, at 69 per cent. However, as a result of the fall in Britain's balance-of-payments deficit between 1989 and 1991, which reduced the net inflow of goods and services from abroad, the resources needed to sustain this level of consumption came (in a national-income accounting sense) mainly from investment (public and private), which fell by 13 per cent over this two-year period. Total investment was only 16 per cent of the GDP in Britain in 1991, compared with 20 per cent in Italy, 21 per cent in France and Germany, and 32 per cent in Japan. In short, consumption in Britain rose too much during the 1980s, at the expense of the balance of payments, and stayed too high at the beginning of the 1990s, at the expense of investment.

The ideal scenario would be one in which rising investment, together with rising exports, led Britain out of recession. But if it is difficult enough to engineer an export-led recovery, it is probably impossible to engineer an investment-led recovery (as far as *private* investment is concerned). More incentives to manufacturing investment should certainly be provided than the exceedingly modest measures announced by Mr Norman Lamont in his 1992 Autumn Statement; but rebuilding Britain's sadly eroded industrial base is going to be a long, slow task, and the main contributor to its achievement must be manufacturing industry's own conviction that the government is committed to bringing the economy back to full employment and keeping it there. Over the past decade and a half it has too often been those businesses which have borrowed and invested, and then found that there was no market for their output, which have gone to the wall. Those that played safe, deciding not to invest or expand, have too often been justified in their pessimism.

Manufacturing investment will also respond to the prospect of a sustained rise in exports, created by a favourable outlook for world trade and a belief that the exchange rate will not be allowed to become overvalued, and that costs can be kept competitive. Substantial investment in new technologies and new products would in turn enhance the competitiveness of British exports. Thus a virtuous circle might be created, with rising exports and rising investment providing encouragement to each other.

Nevertheless, in the circumstances of 1993-4, the part played by exports and private investment in pulling Britain out of recession is likely to be a limited one. The main weight must fall on the government's fiscal policy.

The high import content of consumers' expenditure, coupled with the fact that consumption already represents a dangerously high proportion of GDP, means that the main thrust of expansion (apart from such growth of exports and manufacturing investment as government policies can stimulate) must come from increased public investment. (The fall of over 2 per cent in public investment between 1992–3 and 1993–4 foreshadowed in the statistical supplement to the Chancellor's November 1992 Autumn Statement is an example of the mind-numbing perversity of government policy.) Much of the rise in public investment should take the form of construction projects which can be started quickly and phased out easily once recovery is solidly under way and private investment is rising again; and which have a relatively small direct effect in increasing imports. But a radical shift is also needed in the government's attitude towards public expenditure if Britain is to prosper in the twenty-first century; and now is the time to start. More must be spent by the government on those activities that promote growth of the GDP, and improvements in the quality of life, in the medium to longer term. Expenditure on the nation's physical infrastructure, on research and development, on education and training – all this has been sacrificed over the past decade and a half in the pursuit of policies designed to maximize personal consumption; and this has played a major role in attenuating the country's industrial base and weakening its competitive position. A switch of priorities is overdue, and there is no better time to embark on it than when the economy is in recession, and millions of people have no work to do.

The task is urgent. Britain's ability to produce manufactured goods has already been dangerously diminished. The longer the recession drags on, the greater the damage will be, and the larger the proportion of consumption and investment expenditure which will have to be met by imports – if they can be afforded. The more serious, too, will be the loss of skills and the demoralization of those who have lost their jobs, or fear they may, or have never been able to find a job in the first place.

What is needed is a lot less complacency on the part of those who determine economic policy; and more investment, more exports, more education and training. All this should be within the framework of intelligent management of the level of demand in the economy, of the kind first advocated by Keynes. What is needed is a return to economic sanity.

INDEX

automatic stabilizers, 52

balance of payments
  current account deficits, 20–21,
    58, 123
  inflation, effect of, 38
  North Sea oil, effect of, 9, 58,
    69, 122
  in single European currency,
    108
Bank of England, 56, 65, 116–17
  independence of, 107
Barber, Anthony, 3, 7–8, 23, 47
Black Wednesday, 65–6
  see also Exchange Rate
    Mechanism
borrowing
  government: to balance
    economy, 20; from banking
    system, causing growth of
    money supply, 49–50, 79, 82;
    bonds denoted in foreign
    currencies, 84–5; changing
    government views on, 71;
    debt repayment, 58–9; by
    developing countries, 100–
    101; to finance structural
    deficit, advisability of, 75–6,
    79; index-linked securities,
    83–4; for infrastructure
    projects, 76–7; sale of
    securities to private sector,
    49–50, 80–81; from world
    capital market, 82; see also
    budget deficit; Public Sector
    Borrowing Requirement

private: increase following
  deregulation, 50; mortgage
  debt, 56–8; rapid growth of
  credit, 56–7; see also
  deregulation of financial
  system
Bretton Woods Conference
  (1944), 3, 115
budget
  balanced: abandonment of aim
    (Keynesian view), 20;
    conventional view of, 72–4;
    as Lawson aim, 58;
    monetarist view, 4;
    Thatcher's remedy for
    inflation, 30, 48–9
  deficit: City views as
    inflationary, 82–3; cyclical,
    78, 121–2; deliberate, to
    prevent recession, 20, 52, 63,
    71, 72, 82, 120; financed by
    bonds denoted in foreign
    currencies, 84–5, by
    borrowing, 75–6, 79, by sale
    of index-linked securities,
    83–4, by selling securities,
    79–81; increasing money
    supply, 49–50, 82; and
    Maastricht Treaty, 107;
    structural, 75–8, 120, 1993
    unjustifiable, 78–9
  European Community, 110
  role of, 71–88
  surplus: to dampen economic
    activity, 21, 72; in 1980s,
    58–9

Callaghan, James, 5, 113
Canada, 1
cash limits, 25
City of London, irrational views
    of, 82–4
classical economics, 11–18
    market forces and, 31
    Treasury view, 81
commodity prices
    doubling in 1972–3, 4
    fall 1980–86, 6
    rise 1986–90, 7
construction industry, 86
consumer boom, 58, 123–4
credit, expansion of, as cause of
    recession, 100–103
    see also deregulation of
    financial system

deindustrialization, 51
    see also manufacturing industry
demand management, abandoned
    by Thatcher, 23, 47, 99, 119
    causing inflation, 23–7
    fine tuning, 23
    forecasts, 47
    Friedman on, 25–6, 29
    government's role, 47
    meaning, 21
    need for, 119
    object of, 24
    short-term instruments, 86–7
    use of, post-war, 21–3
Denmark, 9, 106, 110
deregulation of financial system,
    48, 50, 54, 56–7, 59, 101
devaluation
    1967, 2
    1992, 65–7, 116
    to regain competitiveness,
    84
    and single European currency,
    108

ECB (European Central Bank),
    106–7
EMS, see European Monetary
    System
ERM, see Exchange Rate
    Mechanism
education and training, 77–8, 96–
    8
    need for spending on, 126
    to reduce unemployment, 29
    skills deficit, 120–21
    training levies, 96–7
    universities, 97–8
    vocational, 96–7
employment, see unemployment
European Central Bank, 106–7
European Community, economic
    policy in, 85, 106–12
European Monetary System, 55,
    63, 106
    convergence criteria, 106, 107
    and interest rates, 104–5
    sterling as benchmark
    currency, 63
    and unemployment, 108–9
Exchange Rate Mechanism
    Britain's entry, 39, 60–61
    Britain's withdrawal, 33, 39,
    64–5, 105–6
    Major's choice of central rate,
    61
    realignment as soft option, 64–
    5
    retention of, 113–14
    strains in, 64
    Thatcher urged to join, 55
exchange rates
    Bank of England intervention,
    56, 65, 116–17
    and competitiveness, 53, 123
    fixed, inflation's effect on, 38–
    40
    floating, 51, 104–5, 114–15

overvaluation of sterling 1979–
1981, 51
speculators, 116–17
Thatcher's views, 55–6
export-led recovery, 122–4

fine tuning, 23
fiscal policy
expansionary, to cure recession,
20, 71–2, 85–7
Group of Seven, 112
Lamont's, 67–8
stimulus excessive, 58
tight, reducing demand, 52–3,
62
see also Medium Term
Financial Strategy; taxation
forecasts, 47
foreign-exchange control
abolished, 9, 90
foreign-exchange reserves, 56
Fowler, Norman, 97
France
1968 événements, 3
government spending, 22
inflation in, 45, 69
share of consumption in GDP,
123
speculation against franc, 116
top tax rates, 93
see also Group of Seven
Friedman, Milton
on demand management, 25 6
and monetarism, 4
on unemployment, 6

G7, see Group of Seven
GDP, see Gross Domestic Product
Galbraith, J. K., 93
General Theory of Employment,
Interest and Money (Keynes),
12, 119

Germany
Bundesbank, 50, 64, 103–5,
107
competitive exports, 22
hyper-inflation in 1920s, 40
inflation, 69
interest rates, 103–5
low inflation as aim, 45, 103
recession, 103
reunification causing strains,
64, 100, 102–3
share of consumption in GDP,
123
sterling shadowing
Deutschemark, 54–5
top tax rates, 93
vocational training, 97
see also Group of Seven
Gross Domestic Product
defined, 12–13
investment percentage, 124
loss of, due to recessions, 45
ratio of National Debt to, 81
in real terms and money terms,
24, 35–7
saving and investment and, 15–
18
share of consumption in, 123
slow growth of (1979–92), 69
see also manufacturing output
Group of Seven
to control currency speculation,
117
economic summits, 85, 112–13
expansionary policy required,
85, 117, 123
policies exacerbating recession,
1

Healey, Denis, 5
Heath, Sir Edward, 3, 4, 60
housing market, see property
market

How to pay for the war (Keynes), 21

Howe, Sir Geoffrey, 55, 71

incomes
  adjustment of, to ensure equality of saving and investment, 16
  fixed, inflation and, 37–8
  money illusion, 37
  top fifth, 70
  see also prices and incomes policy; wage rates
index-linked securities, 83–4
inflation
  1975, 4, 5
  accelerating, 27–9, 40–42, 46
  balance of payments and, 38
  budget deficit and, 82
  as 'cause of unemployment', 35–7
  causes of: 1970, 2; 1990, 59; monetarist view, 4, 5, 27–9
  cost-push, 41
  defeat of, as main objective, 34
  defined, 34–5
  demand management causing, 23–9
  and ECB, 106–7
  good for economic growth, 42–3
  international comparisons, 69
  money illusion, 37
  not test of successful economic policy, 46
  reasons for fear of, 35–41
  recent phenomenon, 35
  resolving society's tensions, 43
  unemployment, relationship with, 31–2, 45
  zero: as aim, 37–8, 42, 63, 69, 119; costs of achieving, 43–6;

  aim abandoned post Black Wednesday, 66
infrastructure, spending on
  France, 22
  high rate of return on, 76–7
  need for, 86, 125
interest rates
  classical economists on, 14–15
  control of outside EMS, 104
  and 'crowding out', 81–2
  in early 1990s, 62–3
  high: depressing economy, 50–51; increasing M3, 50; inflow of hot money, 51
  Keynes, on, 17–19
  long-term, 63, 82–3
  low: good for economic growth, 43; insufficient to get out of recession, 19, 66, 119–20
  real and nominal distinguished, 62–3, 83
  rise in late 1980s, 60
International Monetary Fund, 5
investment
  in capital goods, 13–15
  equality with saving, 13–14, 16–17
  government action to boost, 104
  incentives needed to increase private, 124
  interest rates, effect of, 19, 104
  not displaced by government sales of securities, 81–2
  public, needed, 125
Italy
  devaluation of lira within ERM, 64–5
  government borrowing, 75
  inflation in, 45
  share of consumption in GDP, 123
  see also Group of Seven

Japan
    expansionary fiscal policy, 111
    exports, 114
    growth of credit, 100–101
    inflation, 69
    share of consumption in GDP,
        123
    stock market collapse, 9
    top tax rates, 93
    see also Group of Seven
Johnson, President Lyndon, 2,
    21
junk bonds, 101

Kahn, Richard, 16
Kennedy, John F., 21
Keynes, John Maynard
    criticism of classical
        economists, 15
    general theory of employment
        explained, 12–20
    on government spending, 88
    see also demand management
Khrushchev, Nikita, 90

Lamont, Norman
    Autumn Statement 1992, 66–8,
        71, 124
    on benefits of ERM, 64–5
    as Chancellor, 8
    fiscal stimulus, lack of, 67–8
    zero inflation abandoned, 66
Lawson, Nigel
    balanced budget as aim, 58
    boom of late 1980s, 3, 7–8
    defeating inflation, 34
    deflationary 1981 budget, 54
    funding deficits, 80
    and Medium Term Financial
        Strategy, 7, 49, 57
    and monetarism, 4–5
    and productivity 'miracle', 94
    shadows Deutschemark, 54–5

    tax cuts, 57–9, 93
Lowe, Robert, 83

MTFS, see Medium Term
    Financial Strategy
Maastricht Treaty, 9, 33, 106–7
    social chapter, 109
MacDougall, Sir Donald, 110
Major, John, 8, 63, 64–6, 113
    joins ERM, 60–61
Malthus, Thomas, 13
manufacturing industry
    decline in output and
        investment, 51, 95
    imports and exports, 53, 58, 94,
        122
    rebuilding manufacturing base,
        124
market forces
    classical economists on, 11–14,
        18, 31
    Keynesian view, 18–19
    Lamont's reliance on, 68
    Thatcher's belief in, 47–8, 55–6,
        89–91, 96
Marshall, Alfred, 11
Medium Term Financial Strategy
    abandonment of, 54, 67
    disastrous effects of, 57
    establishment of, 7–8, 49, 82
    monetary and fiscal aspects of,
        49–53
Mexico, 101
Mill, John Stuart, 11
miners' strike 1973–4, 4
Minford, Patrick, 32
monetarism
    adopted by Thatcher, 5, 30
    essence of, 4–6
    implausibility of, 5–6
    and inflation, 25–30
    jettisoning of aspects of in 1992,
        33

monetarism (*contd*)
   natural rate of unemployment,
      26–32
   rational expectations
      hypothesis, 121
   self-stabilizing economy, 31–3,
      52, 74, 119
money illusion, 37
money supply
   control of: Thatcher's remedy
      for inflation, 30, 48
   correlation with prices, 5–6, 49
   excessive growth of, causing
      inflation, 4, 49, 82
   financing budget deficits, 49–
      50, 79–82
   measures of, 6, 50, 63, 66–7
   monitoring, 66–7
   perverse relationship with
      interest rates, 50
   rapid increases in, 50, 53, 57
   velocity of circulation, 49
mortgage debt, 56–7
multiplier, 16, 20, 86

National Debt, 73, 75, 80–81, 120
National Insurance contributions,
   78, 93
Niehans, Professor, 53

OECD, *see* Organization for
   Economic Cooperation and
   Development
OPEC, *see* Organization of
   Petroleum Exporting
   Countries
oil
   North Sea: and balance of
      payments, 9, 58, 69, 122;
      boosting sterling, 51
   prices, 3, 5, 100
Organization for Economic
   Cooperation and

   Development, 1, 78
Organization of Petroleum
   Exporting Countries
   oil price increases
      1973–4, 4
   surpluses recycled, 100
overseas wealth, 69

PSBR, *see* Public Sector
   Borrowing Requirement
PSDR, *see* Public Sector Debt
   Repayment
poverty, 70, 93
prices and incomes policy
   aim of, 44
   under Labour government, 5,
      25
   need for, 79, 123
   Thatcher's determination to
      avoid, 59–60
   see also wage rates
private investment, *see* investment
privatization of nationalized
   industries, 73, 91–2
productivity
   gains in during 1980s, 9, 93–4
   wages rising faster than, 79
property market
   boom, 56–7
   excessive credit, 100–102
   interest rate rise causing fall, 60
   mortgage-interest tax relief, 78
   over-borrowing, 8
   repossessions, 60
public expenditure
   beneficial effects of, 20, 72, 76–
      8, 81, 86, 96–8, 125
   cuts in, 48, 52–3, 67
Public Sector Borrowing
   Requirement
   defined, 52
   1992 crisis, 62
   following Black Wednesday, 67